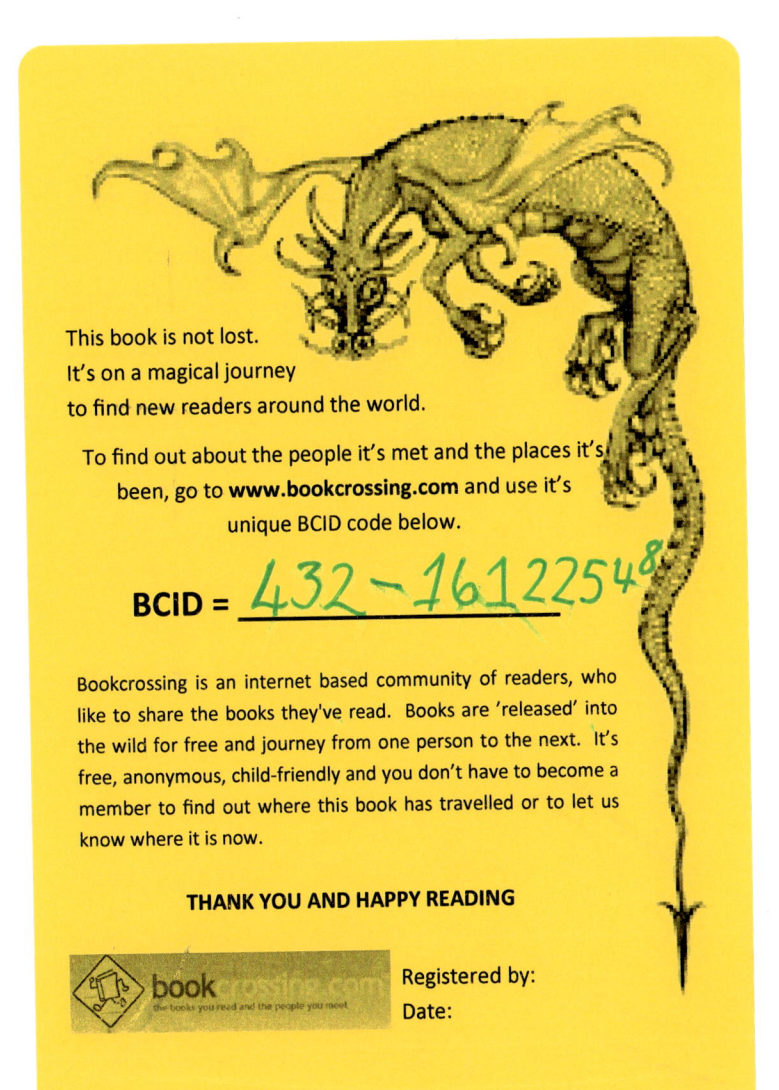

This book is not lost.
It's on a magical journey
to find new readers around the world.

To find out about the people it's met and the places it's been, go to **www.bookcrossing.com** and use it's unique BCID code below.

BCID = 432-16122548

Bookcrossing is an internet based community of readers, who like to share the books they've read. Books are 'released' into the wild for free and journey from one person to the next. It's free, anonymous, child-friendly and you don't have to become a member to find out where this book has travelled or to let us know where it is now.

THANK YOU AND HAPPY READING

Registered by:
Date:

The Business Hen
Raising and Breeding Laying Hens

by Herbert Collingwood

with an introduction by Jackson Chambers

This work contains material that was originally published in 1904.

This publication is within the Public Domain.

This edition is reprinted for educational purposes
and in accordance with all applicable Federal Laws.

Introduction Copyright 2017 by Jackson Chambers

Self Reliance Books

Get more historic titles on animal and stock breeding, gardening and old fashioned skills by visiting us at:

http://selfreliancebooks.blogspot.com/

Introduction

I am pleased to present yet another title on Poultry.

This volume is entitled "The Business Hen" and was published in 1904.

The work is in the Public Domain and is re-printed here in accordance with Federal Laws.

As with all reprinted books of this age that are intended to perfectly reproduce the original edition, considerable pains and effort had to be undertaken to correct fading and sometimes outright damage to existing proofs of this title. At times, this task is quite monumental, requiring an almost total "rebuilding" of some pages from digital proofs of multiple copies. Despite this, imperfections still sometimes exist in the final proof and may detract from the visual appearance of the text.

I hope you enjoy reading this book as much as I enjoyed making it available to readers again.

Jackson Chambers

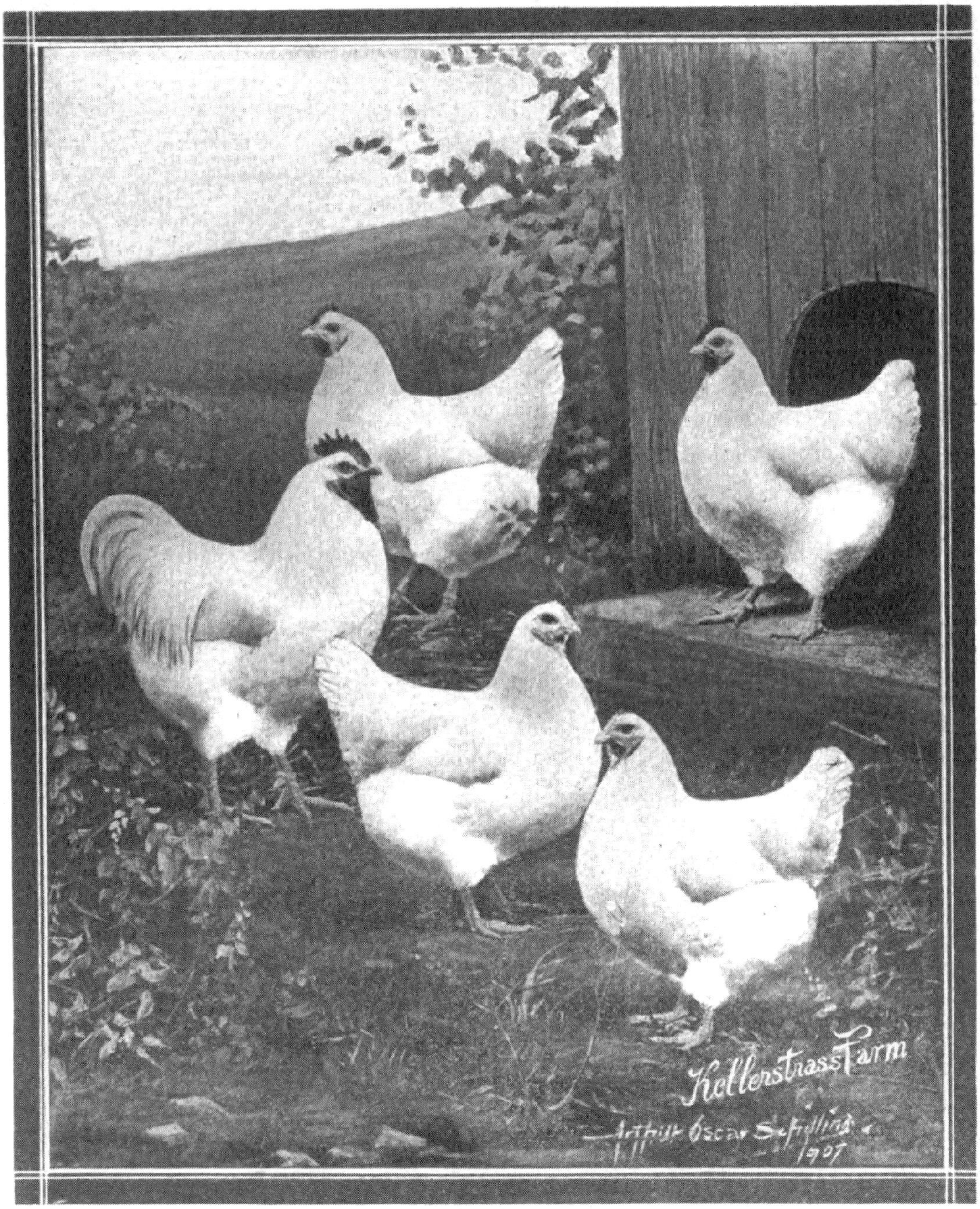
Kellerstrass Farm
Arthur Oscar Schilling
1907

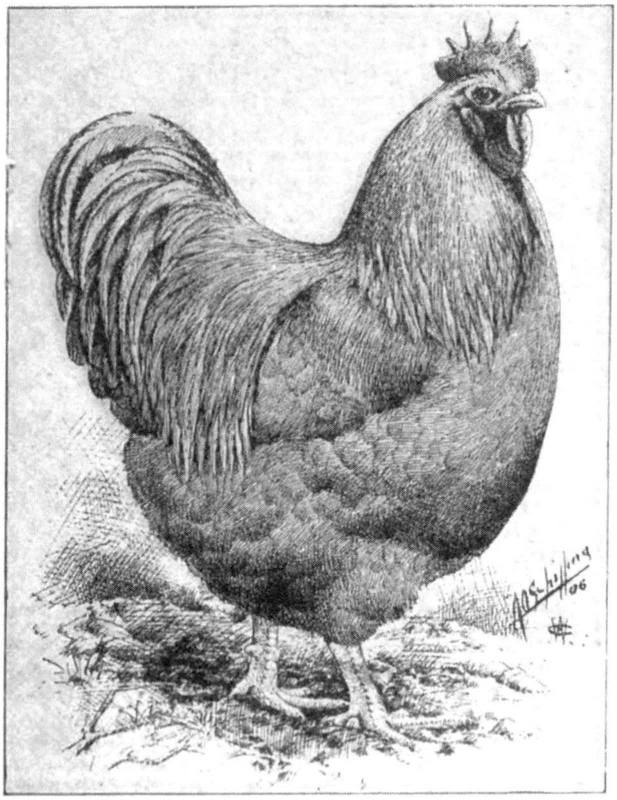

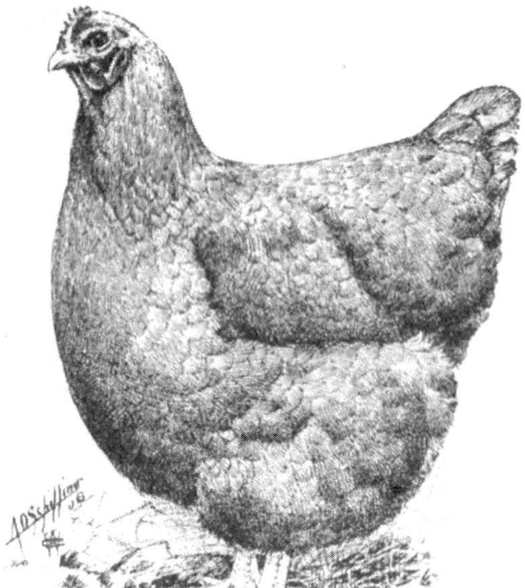

INTRODUCTION

During the past ten years THE RURAL NEW YORKER has given much space to poultry matters. It was necessary to do this in order to answer the thousands of questions asked by readers. These questions were from practical men and women—not fanciers—who asked how to obtain a good hen, and how to feed and care for her in a business-like way. In order to answer these questions we found it necessary to scour the country from one end to the other and to obtain help from hundreds of practical poultry keepers. We find that from year to year many of these questions are repeated—by new readers or by those who have mislaid their papers. This has led us to prepare this book, for it is evident that the information will be far more accessible in book form. These thousands of questions were grouped and analyzed. We then went to the most practical poultry keepers for information. The vast amount of information thus obtained has been sorted, cut down and rewritten to fit into this book. There are of course many details which cannot be crowded into these pages. New conditions are constantly arising, and the most expert poultry keepers are often puzzled by things which they cannot understand. We must all know also that many of the most important things can only be taught by experience. Any reader of THE R. N.-Y. is welcome to ask for further information. We can obtain it for him, and in this way supply all the details which he may need. We have avoided all reference to "big stories" or fancy operations, and attempted to give a statement of methods which practical men have found safe and useful. While hundreds of men and women have helped with experience and advice, I wish to express special thanks to Prof. James E. Rice, who prepared the chapter on "What is an Egg" and "Marketing the Egg" and to Dr. Cooper Curtice, who wrote the article on "Health of the Hen."

H. W. COLLINGWOOD.

CONTENTS

		PAGE.
CHAPTER I	THE BUSINESS BREEDS	5
CHAPTER II	THE SCRUB HEN TURNED TO BUSINESS	10
CHAPTER III	PARENTS OF THE EGG	13
CHAPTER IV	WHAT IS AN EGG?	18
CHAPTER V	HATCHING THE EGG	29
CHAPTER VI	THE CHICKEN'S NURSE	36
CHAPTER VII	CARE OF THE BABY CHICK	40
CHAPTER VIII	THE YOUNG BIRD	45
CHAPTER IX	THE HEN'S HOUSE	49
CHAPTER X	FEEDING THE HEN	58
CHAPTER XI	THE COLONY PLAN	68
CHAPTER XII	THE MARKET GARDENER'S HENS	73
CHAPTER XIII	THE BOY'S HENS	77
CHAPTER XIV	MARKETING POULTRY PRODUCTS	83
CHAPTER XV	MARKETING EGGS	88
CHAPTER XVI	COMPANIONS OF THE HEN	93
CHAPTER XVII	THE HEALTH OF THE HEN	98
CHAPTER XVIII	PUREBRED POULTRY	111
CHAPTER XIX	WHO SHOULD KEEP HENS?	113
CHAPTER XX	ODDS AND ENDS	120

CHAPTER I.

The Business Breeds.

To succeed with poultry, a man must be "half hen." That means that he must love the business and understand the hen. Such a man naturally likes the breed best adapted to his business. There are different kinds of men and thus there are different breeds of poultry, each one best fitted for some special purpose. The keynote of this book is the fact that no man can supply another with that element known as good judgment. We try to give here facts about poultry. The reader is urged to apply them, and learn for himself what will suit him best. Business hens may be roughly classed under three heads,—Mediterranean, or non-sitters; American, or general-purpose breeds which have been obtained by crossing; and Asiatics, or meat-producing breeds. Briefly stated, their business qualities may be described about as follows:

FIG. 1. PUREBRED WHITE LEGHORNS.

MEDITERRANEAN OR NON-SITTERS.—The Leghorn is the best example of this class; a small, nervous hen with a very large comb. The Leghorn, without doubt, is the best breed for those who want an abundance of large, white eggs, or those who want a small flock for a small enclosure. With us the Black Minorca lays a larger white egg, but is more tender, not as hardy as the Leghorn, and requires more feed, though standing confinement better. The Brown Leghorn is smaller than the White, and lays a smaller egg, except some families which have been bred for large eggs. The Brown is thought to be hardier than the White, and with us seems to stand confinement better, and on the whole will lay a few more eggs. The Brown Leghorn, however, is more difficult to breed true to color, and makes a poorer carcass when dressed. The objections to Leghorns are the small size of some families, the large comb, which makes them tender in Winter, and to some extent the fact that the hens rarely sit, so that incubators must be used. The White Leghorns make good broilers, but are too small to make the size of poultry known as roasters. A prominent breeder of Leghorns, speaking of the profit to be made in young White Leghorn roosters, says:

"In eight weeks I can make these birds weigh 3½ pounds per pair. They look like a squab and bring $1.50 per pair. They make a more attractive broiler, are meaty and of high quality. It takes the heavier breeds longer to mature; it costs nearly twice as much to house them, and fully double as much to feed them." One argument in favor of Leghorns, for town lots, is that they occupy less space in houses. A house that will comfortably house 40 Leghorns would be small for 25 Brahmas, or 30 Plymouth Rocks, while eggs are the chief consideration for town poultry. As a rule eggs from the Leghorns are more fertile than those from larger breeds. The young Leghorn hen shown at Fig. 1 laid a clutch of eggs and hatched them before she was five months old.

AMERICAN BREEDS.—This class includes such breeds as Plymouth Rocks, Wyandottes and Rhode Island Reds, produced by crossing older breeds and selecting birds true to a fixed type through a number of years. For example, the Plymouth Rock resulted from crossing the Dominique and the Java with the Brahmas. It is also stated that the Pit Games were used to produce this breed. The Wyandotte came from a non-sitting breed on one side, and

FIG. 2. A 237-EGG PLYMOUTH ROCK.

ought therefore to average better layers. These American breeds have the same general features, plump, well-shaped bodies, clean, yellow legs, and a yellow skin. The English Orpington is much the same general type, but has not yellow skin. This yellow color is important, as the American market calls for yellow meat. These

FIG. 3. A GOOD WHITE WYANDOTTE.

American breeds not only lay well, but also furnish a good carcass of salable meat. They are larger than the Leghorns, consume rather more feed, and do not as a rule lay as many eggs. The eggs of the American breeds are brown in color, and generally not as large as those from the White Leghorns. While brown eggs are preferred in some markets, such as Boston and other New England cities, the general demand is for white eggs. For farm stock where the flock is kept to supply meat and eggs for the farm, with a surplus of each to sell, one of the American breeds will prove very satisfactory. They may be compared with the general-purpose cow, while the Leghorn represents the special-purpose Jersey. Both the Plymouth Rock and Wyandotte are bred in different colors, but the color adds little of value to the breed except the pleasing effect to the eye. The Barred Plymouth Rock is one of the strongest and hardiest of breeds, but the White of both Plymouth Rock and Wyandotte are more popular. Some years ago the flocks in farmers' yards were largely speckled, but now a large proportion of them will be found white. Why is one American breed better than another? The answer will be largely a matter of opinion. A Plymouth Rock breeder, when asked why he prefers that breed to Wyandottes, gives the following answer:

"I do not consider there is much difference between the Wyandottes and the Plymouth Rocks, at least not a contrast as exists between either one of the above and the Leghorn, or such as is between the Leghorn and Cochin. I think which one a person prefers—Wyandotte or Plymouth Rock—is much a matter of fancy, but I consider that there are these differences: First, the Plymouth Rock equals them as layers, but surpasses them in color and size of egg. Second, the Plymouth Rock equals or excels the Wyandotte as a table fowl, and surpasses it in weight. The latter point I consider the strongest. Anyone raising poultry for market, and especially farmers, I think should have the heaviest fowls, provided they are good layers. Good laying and large size are best combined, I think, in the Plymouth Rocks." The picture of a serviceable Barred Plymouth Rock hen is shown at Fig. 2. This hen is known to have laid 237 eggs during her first year.

A Wyandotte breeder, in reply, makes these claims: "White Wyandottes are smaller birds, maturing quicker, commencing to lay two or four weeks earlier than the Plymouth Rocks. I am aware that this will be disputed by Plymouth Rock breeders, especially those with flocks below standard size, and I am willing to admit that Rocks of Wyandotte size may lay as quickly. The White Wyandottes when dressed for market have no dark pin feathers, but show a clear yellow skin, while the Plymouth Rock chicks have a mottled appearance, owing to the coloring matter in the pin feathers. The Wyandottes do not have so deep a breast bone, consequently are rounder breasted and have a meatier look than the P. Rock chicks of the same age. The larger the breed is the longer it takes to reach the egg-laying stage, and in selecting a breed of fowls a man must determine whether a month's earlier production of eggs in November or December isn't worth more than an additional pound of meat, which by the way cannot be produced for nothing, but must be paid for in feed. Another point in favor of the Wyandottes is uniformity of color, without the trouble of special matings for cockerels and for pullets, which are necessary to obtain uniformity in breeding Barred Rocks. This objection does not obtain as against White Plymouth Rocks, of course, but all the other objections hold. Another factor in determining me to change breeds was that my Wyandottes seemed to be much better layers. Against the Wyandottes was the fact that in muddy seasons the plumage would get badly soiled, giving the flock a dirty appearance, not noticed in Barred Plymouth Rocks. As layers the White Wyandottes are not excelled by any other breed except possibly the Leghorns, and in Winter months, under similar conditions, I think they will surpass the Leghorns." The White Wyandotte shown at Fig. 3 laid 219 eggs in her first season, and kept up her record later.

THE ASIATICS.—The Light Brahma is the most popular type of this class, a large, slow, well-feathered and well-shaped bird, quiet in disposition, laying a fair number of dark brown eggs. The legs are well feathered, the comb small, and the hens seem well dressed in fur for Winter work. The Brahmas and Cochins are docile and stand confinement well, but they fatten readily, and it is harder to keep them free from vermin than the lighter and thinner-feathered breeds. The feathers on the legs are objectionable in damp or muddy situations. We are more likely to overfeed the larger breeds, and make them too fat for good layers. The good points of the Brahma are fairly stated by a leading poultryman as follows:

"The Light Brahma is a very tame breed; will bear close confinement and do well. They may be kept in a yard with a fence three feet high, made of wire netting. The chicks will grow very fast; at the age of six months they will weigh seven pounds, and will bring the highest market price, because they have nice yellow meat and are well fattened. I sold my chickens last Fall, and they brought me 18 cents per pound dressed. I can fatten them up quicker than the lighter breeds. They are just the breed for the city. They are one of the oldest breeds, and have come to stay. They are good layers for Winter and Summer, good sitters and mothers. For an all-'round breed they cannot be beaten. My objection to the smaller breeds is that I live in a village and have not the room. Any one who has little room ought not to keep Leghorns or the like. They need more run, and more run means more feed. A breed that does not run requires less feed, and that is the light Brahma."

The Cochins and Brahmas have yellow legs and skin, while Langshans, another Asiatic breed, have dark legs and white skin. There are many other excellent breeds, such as Polish, Hamburg, Orpingtons, Redcaps, Javas, Houdans and others. Some of them are profitable in the hands of breeders who know and love them, but we do not class them here as business hens. The Orpingtons are said to represent a cross between the Langshans and the Minorcas. They are classed as excellent layers and are gaining in popularity. They lack the yellow skin which is a strong feature of the American breeds. The Dorkings are large birds, fair layers, and good mothers, perhaps the first of all table fowls, but not as hardy as others. The Games are active birds, and while of little value for business, when bred pure are often useful to cross with other breeds, especially when the birds are to run at large on a farm. The half-bred Games make good foragers and fair layers, and are able to defend themselves against vermin. A half-bred Game hen has been known to fly into the air and fight with a hawk in defense of her chicks. It is often asked if the new colors which are constantly appearing in all breeds add anything of practical value. It is safe to say that there is nothing in the color of the plumage of any of the varieties (or strains), of the several breeds that indicate superiority. The color is barely skin deep. Each variety has its admirers, and each is claimed as something better than the others. We have not found color to add merit to a breed, and the only difference between varieties of the same breed is that the colors are not alike. Breeds that are not very numerous are sometimes lacking in hardiness by reason of being inbred, but this applies only to Javas, Dorkings, Polish, Hamburgs, Redcaps, etc.

CHAPTER II.

The Scrub Hen Turned to Business.

By "scrub" is meant the hen that runs in the barnyard, roosts in a tree in Summer, and either in the barn or in some broken henhouse in Winter. She is usually of no particular breed. She leaves her mark over the machinery, scratches up the garden, when there is any, and keeps busy generally. She is not fed regularly. Sometimes the farmer throws out a little corn, or the women save some table scraps from dog or cat, but the hen lives for the most part on what she can pick up around the barn and yard; clover chaff, grain dropped by the stock, anything that her sharp eyes can find. In Summer, when insects abound, the scrub hen balances her ration better than a chemist could do it for her. A grain of corn, a bug, a blade of grass, a nip out of a ripe tomato, a worm or a bit of ground feed that the horse dropped out of his mouth, fill the scrub hen's crop to overflowing. When lice worry her she rolls in the dust and deserts her so-called house. She can usually clear herself of all but head lice in this way. Roup and cholera trouble her little—her outdoor life keeps her strong and well. She has the reputation of being a mighty layer, because she does about all her laying in the Spring and early Summer, and makes a big fuss about is. She rarely lays 50 eggs during the year. No one keeps her record. Without care she will go back to the condition of her ancestors, who only laid eggs enough to fill a nest, like the other wild birds. She finds her own nest, for those man fixes for her are not to her taste. Sometimes she sits on her eggs for several days before they are picked up, regardless of the fact that before two days of incubation are over the heart of the little chick inside the egg can be plainly seen. The scrub hen is not responsible for the fact that thousands of such eggs are sent to market to disgust those who ought to buy more eggs! During the Winter the scrub hen quits, and gives a fair imitation of a woodchuck living on his fat. No one can blame her! She has all she can do to keep life in her body, to say nothing of laying eggs! Many of these scrub hens would, if they had the chance, rank well as layers, with some of the purebreds, but what can a hen do without a chance?

In spite of all, many of these flocks of scrub hens are profitable. It costs little or nothing to feed them in Summer, and the eggs they lay and the meat they furnish are nearly all clear gain. They usually deprive the family of a good garden, for few men who will not care for a flock of poultry will ever build a fence that will keep them out of the garden. Through the Winter they are usually an expense and little more. The ordinary flock of scrub poultry contains a large number of surplus roosters—too many for any practical use. Lice, starvation, lack of shelter and surplus roosters are the chief reasons why many of these worthy hens remain scrubs. In every such flock there is the foundation for a class of poultry that will be a credit to the farm, and pay better in proportion to value than any other stock. If the farmer does not care for the job of improvement some woman or child may well take hold of it.

What can be done?

The flock is probably inbred—that is, all of one family. Kill off all the roosters and eat or sell them. Pick out 15 or 20 of the best of the hens, and make some good-sized yard where they can have a good run. Make up your mind what class of poultry you want to breed, and then buy a Leghorn, a Wyandotte or a Plymouth Rock rooster from some good breeder. Don't go to a neighbor and "swap roosters," but get a bird that cannot be closely related to your hens. If you can pick out yearling hens, buy a young rooster. If the hens are younger buy an older male. Put him with your selected hens, and use those eggs for setting. You need no other rooster on the farm. If the flock is small you may not want to pen up the selected hens, but unless you do you cannot be sure that your eggs for hatching will be what you want. The improvement made in one season by the use of a good male on selected hens is often surprising. If you can do so, buy one or two settings of eggs of the same breed as the rooster, and hatch them under your hens. Get them from different breeders. Then you can select a good rooster from the chicks for the next year's breeding. As soon as the young roosters are large enough to kill sell or eat them. Keep only one good one on the farm—with your best hens. Do not let the hens hatch where the other hens lay, or send them off to steal their nests. You must control such things if you expect to improve your stock. Find some old building or room, clean it up and handle the sitting hens as described elsewhere in this book. It will take more time to give the hens and chicks this care, but it will pay, as many a farmer's wife has found. When cold weather comes, a warm house will be absolutely necessary. This does not mean an expensive building, but a shelter of any kind where the hens may be comfortable. In parts of the West a frame of poles is set up and covered with straw in November. The hens run inside this warm shelter and do well. In May the straw is taken away and burned, or used for the garden. The success with such rude shelter shows that it is not so much the kind of house, but the warmth and freedom from drafts, frost, lice and foul air that makes the hen think that Spring has come in February. On every farm where there are hens there is some old henhouse. Clean it up and try it. Go at it with hoe and boiling water, and make it clean! Take out the roosts, paint them with kerosene, and swab out the cracks and corners. Make a thick whitewash, add a little carbolic acid to it, and smear the whole inside over. An old house is alive with lice, and you should kill them all before you force a hen to stay there. Before cold weather comes make that house tight. Either tack paper all around inside or put up lath or wire and stuff in straw. Keep drafts away from the hens. Study what is said about house building and feeding, and come as near to it as you can. The chief object of this book is to show how others have succeeded with hens. The scrub grows into the true Business Hen by the application of business principles which mean work, care and patience. You must work these general rules out to suit your own case. Do not be satisfied with the scrub that lays 50 eggs, but give her children the breeding and care that will make them lay 150 eggs.

The history of one of our best American breeds, the Rhode Island Red, will show a farmer what an ordinary hen may come to if well handled. By carefully selecting his best hens and crossing them with an Asiatic breed, a Rhode Island farmer obtained a class of poultry which became noted for egg production and meat value. Others took up the hens, and from them developed the Rhode Island Reds, which are considered by many as strong rivals of the Wyandottes. The breed has not yet been 'fixed"—that is, specimens will not breed as true in color or habits as a breed like the Plymouth Rock. Its future will depend upon the breeders who perfect it. If they favor large egg production, they will select hens with that object in view and thus we shall have a smaller and more active bird than the Light Brahma or even the Plymouth Rock. We speak of this to show how a breeder may control the character of his poultry.

Another thing connected with improvement of the scrub hen is the moral or civilizing effect it will have upon the family. The effect upon any household of changing a lot of neglected mongrels into a flock of handsome and uniform hens cannot help being beneficial. It will create a new interest in farming and lead to efforts to improve the larger stock on the farm. If some bright boy can be put in charge of the work and given a fair chance to develop the hens you will begin to train a good farmer while improving the flock. On some farms the boy often has a colt or a calf or pig to call his own, though he does not always get the money for it. For many reasons a good flock of poultry would be much better for him, and it would be hard to think of any better training for such a boy than the patience and skill required to turn a scrub into a "Business Hen."

CHAPTER III.

Parents of the Egg.

The egg contains the future chick. It may be said to carry the character of the parents wrapped up in a shell. Having selected the breed that is best suited to his wants and conditions, the poultry keeper of course wants the best specimens of that breed that he can produce. It is far better to stick to one breed and select a definite type than to cross breeds.

PEDIGREE.—We know that with all animals, from cats to cattle, there are good and bad specimens in every breed. We call some cows better than others because the good ones give more milk than the poor ones. We do not from choice raise calves from cows that we know are poor ones. If we raise calves at all we save the daughters of the best cows in the herd, because we feel sure that some of the good qualities of the mother will be handed down to the daughter. We know that such things as color and shape are carried in this way, and that character goes along with them. If the mother is reasonably sure to give something of her character to her daughter she is more likely to do so if her own mother and ancestors, for several generations, have been selected for a similar purpose. That is what we call "pedigree" in live stock, and improvement in the character of the cow or the hen comes through our ability to make the daughter better than the mother. The way to do this is to select the best mothers for breeding.

How are we to know them?

A good dairyman can pick out a first-class milker by her shape and various points which he can see or feel. His eye will enable him to make a good guess, but he would not raise a calf from one of these cows until he had a fair idea of how much milk she can give, or what her mother did. Most men who try to improve their poultry must depend on the eye for selecting breeding stock. They make up their mind what size, shape and color will suit them. When that is fixed in mind they have a "type," and they will naturally cull out the birds that fall short of it. By watching their hens and observing their habits they soon find that they can pick out the layers, just as they learn to separate the workers from the shirks in men or in children. They find that the laying hen *acts* like a worker. She is busy and active—off the roost early in the morning after food—a picture of nervous energy. The lazy hen is slow to leave the roost, and shows by her actions that she takes little interest in the things that attract the layer. We cannot describe the "points" of a layer. A man must study them for himself. Mr. C. H. Wyckoff, who selected his White Leghorn breeding hens by the eye—studying shape and what egg-laying habits he could see—said that when he finally made his selection he found the hens about as follows:

EGG TYPE.—"Large-boned, rather long in leg and neck, long on the back, deep up and down, with legs set fairly well apart, breast bone somewhat prominent, flesh hard, strong and muscular, in good condition, but not fat; comb rather above average in size; eyes bright and full; disposition lively, but not scarey; more inclined to follow after and crowd about than to run and fly; large consumers of food, and always hungry when fed regularly and given a chance to exercise."

Of course the type for other breeds would differ from this, but the owner must first decide what he wants his hens to be, and then watch for that type in his flock. In most breeds the best layers are broad and deep, with rather long bodies, with a long neck and small head. The shape of the hen is not as safe a guide as with other animals, for the hen is covered with feathers which may seem to change her shape. The *actions* of the hen indicate her laying qualities far better than her shape; still it is well to fix a certain type in mind and use it for our standard. Strong and vigorous chicks cannot be hatched unless the hens are in good condition. If they are fat and dumpy the chicks will fail. The hens must be kept at work and in good condition.

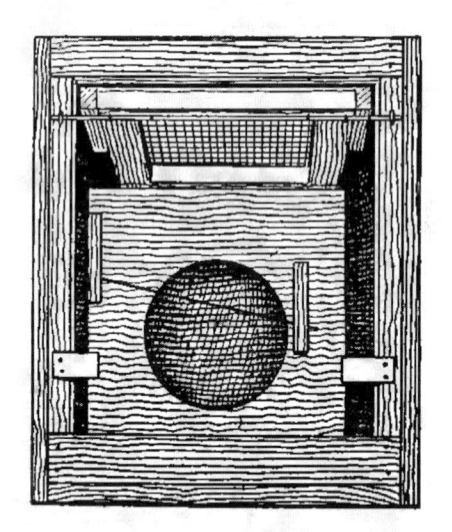

FIG. 4. TRAP NEST OPEN.

SELECTING BREEDERS.—When a man is keeping poultry for profit, or expects to continue in the business, he should keep these selected breeders by themselves with the best male bird he can find. In this way he can use the eggs from these hens for hatching. Usually he will have to select the male by his appearance, but he should try to have him close to the general type of the hens, and be sure that he is strong, vigorous and active. It is not a wise plan to select these breeders in the Spring, just before their eggs are wanted for hatching. All hens are laying them, the lazy as well as the good ones, and the hen that lays 50 eggs a year may make more fuss while she is actually working than the one that lays 150. We should watch the hens through the season, and make the selection during the late Summer and Fall, when most of them stop.

TRAP NESTS.—There is a way of picking the robbers from the workers by using what are called "trap nests." Two of such nests are shown here. The nest is a box with the door so adjusted that when the hen goes in to lay this door closes and shuts her in. She cannot get out until some one opens the door. Each hen has a band on her leg carrying a number, and by marking her number on the egg she has laid, it is possible to know what each hen in the pen is doing. Those who use these trap nests tell some remarkable stories about their results. They have picked out hens by the eye and found by testing that some of them laid twice as many eggs as others. It is claimed that by testing hens with the trap nests and using eggs from the best for hatching, through several generations, an "egg-laying strain" of great value can be developed. The plan is not generally practiced, however. Most breeders think it requires too much time. The hens sometimes refuse to enter the nests and lay outside. It is also claimed that the egg-laying habit alone is not a safe guide, but that the shape and vigor of the birds must be considered. The "trap nest" at least gives a chance for selecting a male bird of good "pedigree." For the average poultry keeper the best advice is to pick out a type and study the habits of the hens. Then select by the eye hens enough to supply the eggs needed for hatching. We would especially study the actions of the pullets as they begin to lay.

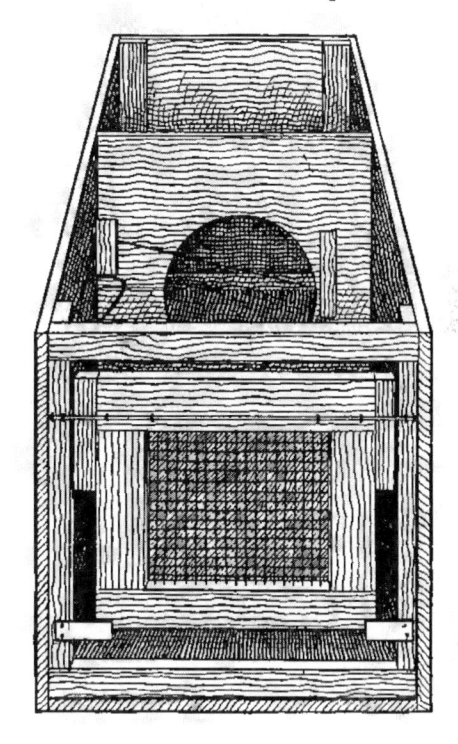

FIG. 5. TRAP NEST SHUT.

CARE OF BREEDERS.—These breeders should be given as large a run as possible, for exercise is necessary if we expect healthy chicks. Yearling hens are selected for breeders with a younger male. There are several good reasons why pullets are not used for breeding stock by experienced poultrymen. They begin laying earlier than the older hens, so that when eggs are most wanted for incubators the pullets have been laying steadily for a long time. Such eggs are not so likely to be fertile as those laid earlier in the laying period and the chicks from them will be weaker. We want eggs from the hen in her full vigor, not after she has been exhausted by long laying. The pullets too are young and not fully matured, and thus not so likely to produce the best chicks. The older hens lay fewer eggs, which are likely to be stronger. If pullets are used an older male should be put with them, while a vigorous young bird is better for the older hens. The number of hens to the male will vary with the breed and the size of the flock. For the heavier breeds 15 hens are enough, while we have known cases where one male to 50 Leghorn hens gave a large per cent of fertile eggs. For the smaller breeds we prefer an average of 25 hens. In some cases two males are used alternately in a small flock. One will run with the hens for four or five days, while the other is kept in a small cage. Then the caged bird will be set free and his rival put in the cage. This double system is more likely to insure fertile eggs, but of course the two males must be alike in type. Some successful poultrymen pay little attention to selecting breeders, but take eggs from large flocks where several males are kept together. Such men say that proper feeding will make any hen lay, but unless hens are quite different from all other animals their character is largely made by inherited qualities.

We give considerable space to this matter, because it is the foundation of improvement in the flock of poultry. The proper selection and mating of the parents of the egg may mean a difference of 50 per cent in hatchable eggs and raisable chicks. In some farm flocks little attention is paid to improvement by selection—the plea being that it takes too much time to bother with such things, though a child might easily be interested in it. Even in such cases it will pay to have a certain type in mind, and cull out for eating purposes the birds that fall short of this standard. We may undo most of our work of breeding by selection if we do not bring in "new blood" from time to time. Some good flocks are ruined by what is known as "inbreeding"—that is, breeding brothers and sisters or closely related members of the same family. We can obtain "new blood" by buying a good male bird from some breeder, or several sittings of eggs.

From the chicks hatched from these eggs we should be able to pick two or more good males to head our breeding pens; above all things, be sure to select strong and vigorous stock. When we buy such eggs or birds we buy a share of the skill and patience which other breeders have spent in selecting. We may thus buy for a dollar results which would cost us five years of personal study and work.

CROSSING THE BREEDS.—Mr. P. H. Jacobs says that it is the common belief among many that to mate individuals of different breeds is to insure greater vigor and hardiness, as well as avoid inbreeding. Such a system among poultrymen is termed "crossing." Before crossing for "vigor" it would be well first to ascertain whether the flock is lacking in that respect, and, if so, the safer method would be to discard the individuals and replace them with others of the same breeds. All breeds are the result of careful and judicious crossing, and any attempt to improve a flock of purebred fowls by crossing is to incur the risk of destroying all the desirable characteristics obtained only after years of patient industry and skillful selection.

"It should not be overlooked that each breed possesses only one dominant trait, or talent. It may combine several desirable characteristics, but it will excel in one only. No breed is perfect, as it will surely be found lacking in some respect. For instance, the prolificacy of certain breeds may be offset by lack of hardiness, exceedingly large combs, very small size, inability to endure confinement, etc., while the breeds preferred in market may not equal some others as layers.

"When two purebred fowls are crossed—that is, when birds of different breeds are mated—such breeding cannot possibly add to the progress more than is possessed by the parent individuals. The crossing of Leghorn and Brahma fowls does not prove beneficial, for the reason that such a cross is not only what may be termed a 'violent' one, but the progeny is not a nonsitter, like its Leghorn parent, does not possess greater activity than the Leghorn, nor it is as hardy as the Brahma, losing in size as well as in adaptability to exist under the same conditions as either parent. A cross of Hamburg and Leghorn (within non-sitting breeds) made by me, produced progeny with persistent inclination to become broody, while every attempt to secure vigor, hardiness, improved market quality, or prolificacy, by crossing dozens of breeds, in various matings and selections, has always failed to give me satisfactory results. It is better to rely upon pure breeds, and select them especially for the purpose one may have in view, as each breed will be found adapted for accomplishing certain objects more than others.

FIG. 6.
"CHEAP JOHN" TRAP NEST.

"Crossing is always disastrous to him who abandons the pure breeds. The next generation (if the cross-bred fowls are used) produces nondescripts, having no uniformity of color, size, or characteristics, seemingly reverting to all the ancestors in their breeding, the whole being a motley lot, on a par with scrubs. The first cross of two purebred fowls usually shows the progeny to resemble the male parent in general appearance, rather than the female, and the points of excellence of the parents are lost rather than intensified. My experience has been that no one has ever attempted the crossing of pure breeds who did not eventually find his flock composed of scrubs, and crossing has done more to disgust admirers of poultry than anything else, as by so doing they destroy the beauty of their flocks and gain nothing from a utilitarian standpoint. If one wishes to add vigor and hardiness to the members of his flock he can do so by procuring males from other well-known sources, while even the common flock may be improved by the use of purebred males every year."

CHAPTER IV.

What is an Egg?

The egg is the first stage in the reproduction of birds. Its function primarily is to produce offspring, secondarily to furnish food for the embryo and for man. The hen therefore fulfills dual purposes which in a measure are antagonistic in their requirements. The first demand of nature is that the hen shall produce eggs that possess all the qualities of life and nutrition necessary to produce strong chickens; the second, that she shall furnish eggs good to eat and lots of them. In order to satisfy the commercial requirements of man the hen often is compelled to sacrifice the higher demands of nature. It becomes a vital question therefore for every poultryman to decide to what extent he can force heavy laying without sacrificing the fertility of the eggs or the vitality of the chickens. It is well, then, that we inquire what an egg is and how it is formed.

HOW THE EGG IS MADE.—The first stage in the development of the egg is the formation of the "yolk." The "ovary" or "egg cluster," which forms a part of the muscular tissue on the left side of the spine, contains many yolks in various stages of development, depending upon the condition of the hen, from the full-sized ripe yolk ready to be detached, to the microscopic cells so small that they cannot be discerned by the naked eye. Within this ovarian tissue is the power to develop countless other yolks not yet apparent. The number of these yolks or "ova," which may be developed, is not a fixed quantity, certainly not exactly 600, as is frequently stated. The number of eggs which a hen will lay depends upon the inherited tendency of each hen to reproduce, and upon her vigor and vitality to withstand the heavy drain upon her system. The ovary of certain hens is absolutely sterile. Others have the power to produce a few eggs in short litters, while some have an ovary so strong and reproductive that they lay almost without interruption, and continue to do so for years. The egg-laying power is a matter of inheritance. It is a question of selection and breeding, and of stimulating the ovaries to activity by proper feeding.

Fig. 1, next page, shows ovary of a hen; 2 is the yolk held within the ovisac or follicle (5). When the yolk is fully ripe it bursts from the follicle and drops into the neck of the oviduct (7). Here we see a wise provision of nature. In order to prevent rupture of blood vessels where the follicle opens, there is a suture mark around the entire surface, where the blood vessels meet but do not cross (4). If for any reason the folli-

What Is An Egg? 19

cle is ruptured before it is matured, through rough handling of the fowl or because of weakness due to debility, a slight clot of blood escapes, which remains on the surface of the yolk or mingles with the white, which leads the consumer to suspect an egg which is perfectly fresh to have been slightly incubated. Occasionally, when hens are in perfect laying condition, two yolks will ripen and burst their follicles at the same time,

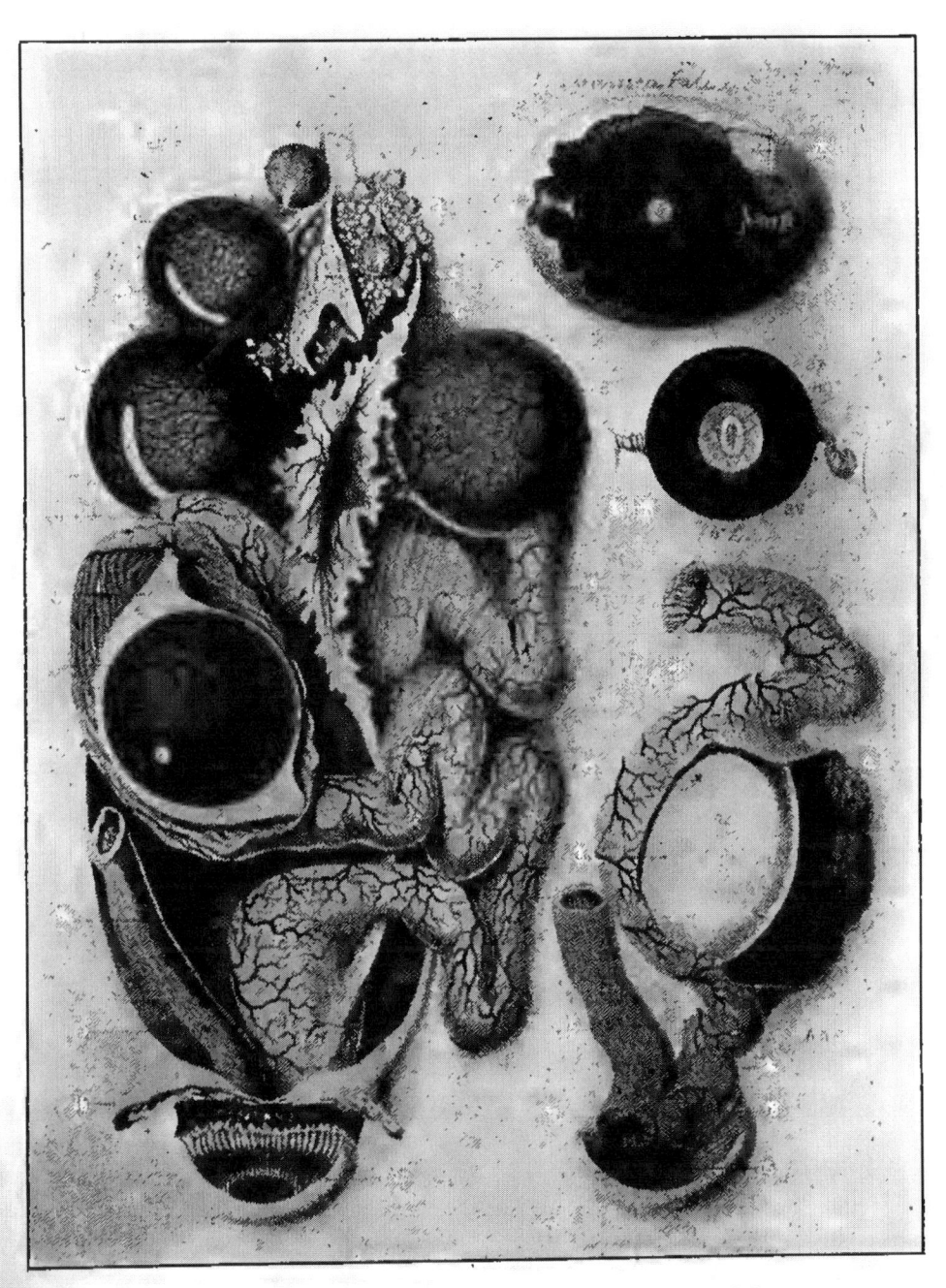

FIG. 7. DEVELOPMENT OF A HEN'S EGG.

and be encased within the same shell, producing a double yolked egg. It is perfectly apparent then that if the yolk is the first part of the egg to be formed that all the conditions for its development must be met, or the hen cannot make the egg. The activity of development of the ovary depends first upon good health. The hen in the best laying condition is in the best health. Reproduction is a question of nerve strength which is dependent upon physical vigor. The over-fat hen does not lay well, because over-fatness is softness and weakness, which ends in debility. A poor hen cannot lay because there is no surplus fat with which to make the egg. Analysis of the yolk of an egg shows it about one-half fat. Unless the fowl can supply the available fat the yolk cannot develop. Therefore it will be found that the hens in their best laying condition will have a little surplus fat in their body.

When the yolk has entered the oviduct it is quickly passed along where the albumen or "white" is deposited (10). During the passage it is pushed forward by the contraction of the muscles of the oviduct, which, being twisted and convoluted, gives the yolk a turning motion as it advances, so that the albumen is deposited in several layers. These layers may be seen by examining carefully a hard-boiled egg. The twisting motion of the yolk in its passage causes twisted string-like fibres of albumen to form on two sides of the yolk. These are called the "chalazæ," Fig. 3 (5). They cause the yolk to swing in the watery albumen like a hammock. This tends to prevent injury to the yolk by any jarring or jolting which the egg may receive.

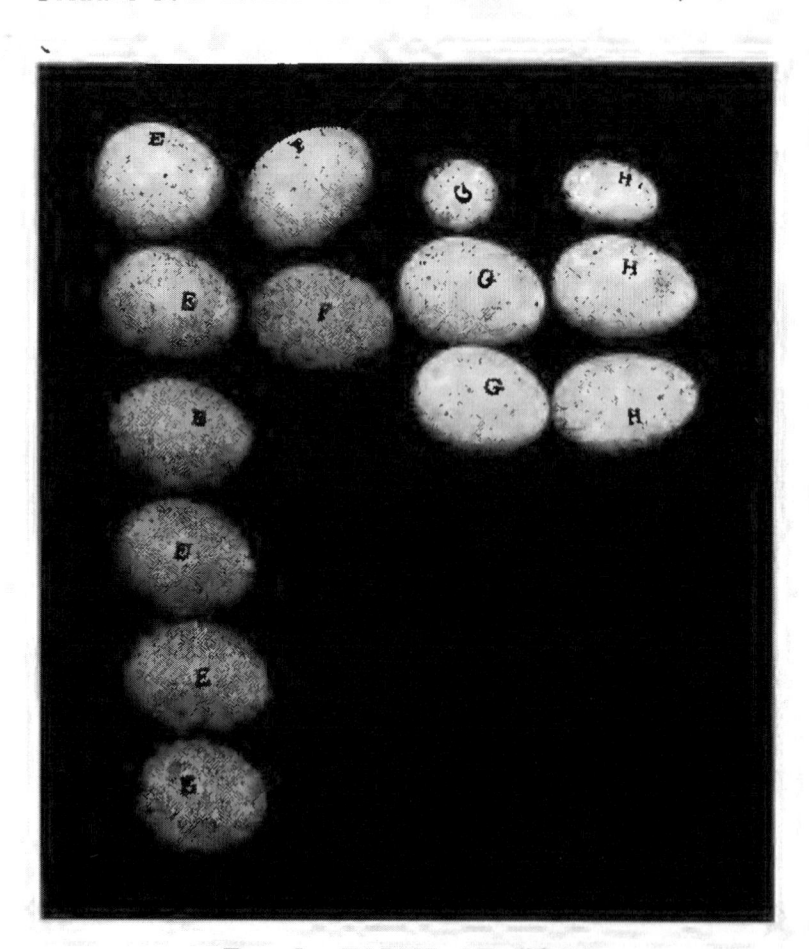

FIG. 8. FORMS OF EGGS.

Whatever way the egg is turned the yolk quickly assumes its natural position. The yolk, containing a large amount of fat, is lighter than the albumen, therefore has a tendency to float at the surface, which during incubation allows the young germ of life, which is on the surface of the lightest portion of the yolk, to float in the warmest portion of the egg, which is in contact with the body of the incubating hen.

The yolk is covered by the "vitelline" membrane (11). The yellow liquid within the membrane is called the "vitellus," which is used for the most part to nourish the young chicken just before and for several days after it hatches. The color of the yolk depends upon the kind of food fed. Yellow corn and green food produce a deep colored yolk, while oats, wheat and buckwheat produce a light yellow, due to the absence of coloring pigment in the grain. One of the first signs of weakened vitality in hens is a tenderness of the vitelline membrane, which often ruptures when eggs are roughly handled. This allows the vitellus to escape and mingle with the white. The yolks therefore of perfectly fresh eggs from such hens will rupture even when the egg is carefully broken. Keeping eggs weakens the vitelline membrane.

Just under the vitelline membrane, and at the surface of the yolk, is the "germinal vesicle," Fig. 1 (12), the vital life principle of the egg. Without fecundation by the male no life would be developed in the germinal vesicle, and the egg would be infertile. If fecundation should take place and the hen should not be in vigorous condition, life would not necessarily be developed. Infertility is due quite as much to lack of vital force of the hen, because of close confinement, excessive laying or improper feeding as to any fault of the male.

Fecundation cannot take place until the yolk has burst from the tough skin of the follicle, Fig. 1 (5), has entered the oviduct, Fig. 1 (7). Here it comes in contact with the "spermatozoa" of the male, which there swarm and live for several weeks, growing less numerous and less active with age. The spermatozoa penetrate the vitelline membrane, unite with the germinal vesicle and life is begun. If the egg should be retained for any considerable time, which often happens, the body heat will start the process of incubation, which will continue until the egg is placed in a temperature too cold for development. Eggs which are not fertile will therefore continue without danger of incubation in a temperature that would allow life to develop with a fertile egg.

After the albumen has been secreted in the part of the oviduct, Fig. 1 (9), it is pushed along to a point where the shell membrane is formed, it is supposed somewhere at or between 13—14 Fig. 1, after which another membrane is added. Then the egg passes to position marked 14 Fig. 1, and Fig. 2 (2), where the glands secrete a liquid which contains carbonate of lime and other mineral matters. This hardening process is completed frequently while the hen is on the nest. A color pigment is sometimes secreted with the shell-making liquid, which gives to eggs their characteristic colors. The color of the shell is largely an individual characteristic, and remains practically constant with the individual, except that the egg shell gradually fades in color toward the end of the laying period. This is particularly noticeable in comparing the first and the last eggs laid by turkeys. The shell-making fluid appears to be secreted by tiny ducts, which leave their impression by numerous fine depressions or pores in the egg shell, which can be easily seen by close inspection. The importance of providing mineral matter in the form of cracked oyster shell, mortar and bone is seen in the fact that if the hen lacks these materials or through debility cannot assimilate them, her eggs will be soft-shelled. Naturally, when the egg production has drained her system of this material, her appetite craves it, and if it is not otherwise supplied, she will instinctively eat the egg shells. This is the most common cause of egg eating.

When the egg rests in the "cloaca," Fig. 2 (4), before being laid, it is covered with a secretion that assists in the depositing of the egg, which when dry gives the shell its natural fresh appearance, and which undoubtedly has much to do with controlling the evaporation of the egg contents. Therefore eggs for hatching should not be washed unless it be to remove dirt which would materially stop the pores in the shell. This oily coating is particularly apparent on duck eggs.

It is to be doubted whether a hen can voluntarily stop the formation of an egg up to the point of its completion. But she can retain the egg at will for considerable time thereafter. It is perfectly certain, however, that improper feeding, neglect, fright or any condition that interferes with digestion or peace of mind will stop the process of egg-making in any of its stages. Frequently the white is deposited without yolk or shell. It is very common to find eggs devoid of shell, and occasionally a yolk will be laid without shell or albumen. It is not uncommon to find an egg with white and shell complete without the yolk. In rare instances a perfect egg has been found within an egg. This is brought about by the completed egg being forced back by injury through the portion of the oviduct where additional albumen is secreted and then returning to the place where a new shell is deposited. When the egg evaporates, the outer membrane, Fig. 3 (3), continues to adhere to the shell, while the inner membrane follows the contents of the egg as it shrinks in size, thus forming the air space, which is usually at the large end of the egg, occasionally on the side and rarely on the small end.

The shape of the egg is determined by the form of the mold in which it is cast, which differs with breeds, varieties, and even with individuals of the same strain. The form of egg peculiar to an individual remains practically constant, so much so that one can pick out an egg from certain hens from a large flock with quite a degree of certainty, purely by the shape of the egg. The groups of eggs shown in Figs. 8-11 show this point very accurately. The eggs marked (a) were laid by hen No. 56; those at (b) by hen No. 148, both White Wyandottes; those at (c) by hen No. 70; those at (d) by hen No. 75, both Single Comb White Leghorns;

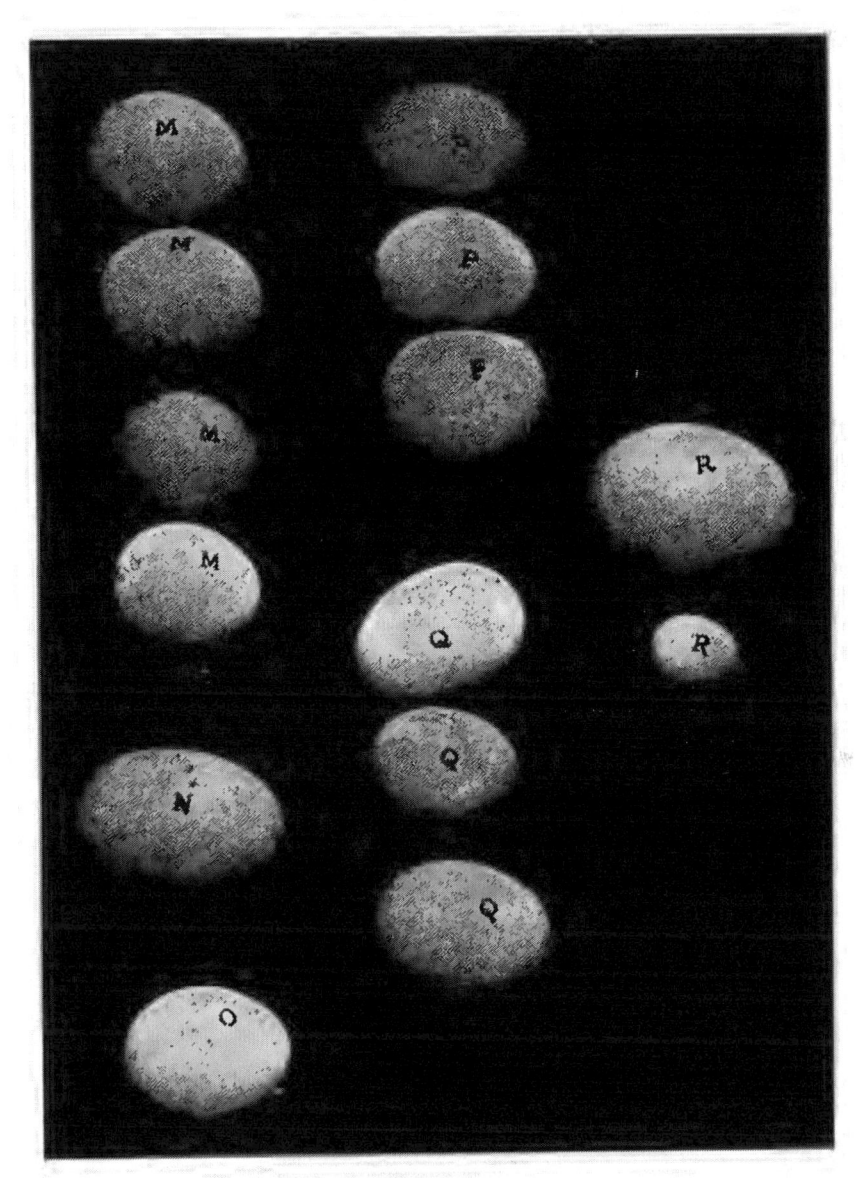

FIG. 9. FORMS OF EGGS.

those at (e) were laid by a White Plymouth Rock; those at (f) by a Barred Plymouth Rock. It will be seen that each hen has a type of egg which is peculiarly her own, differing only slightly from day to day, except in a case of abnormality due to some unusual condition. The eggs

24 *The Business Hen.*

marked a, b, c, and d, were picked out of a large tray full of eggs which were laid by different hens. The selection was made strictly upon their shape and color without looking at the number of the hen, which is marked on the large end of the egg when it is gathered. The peculiar

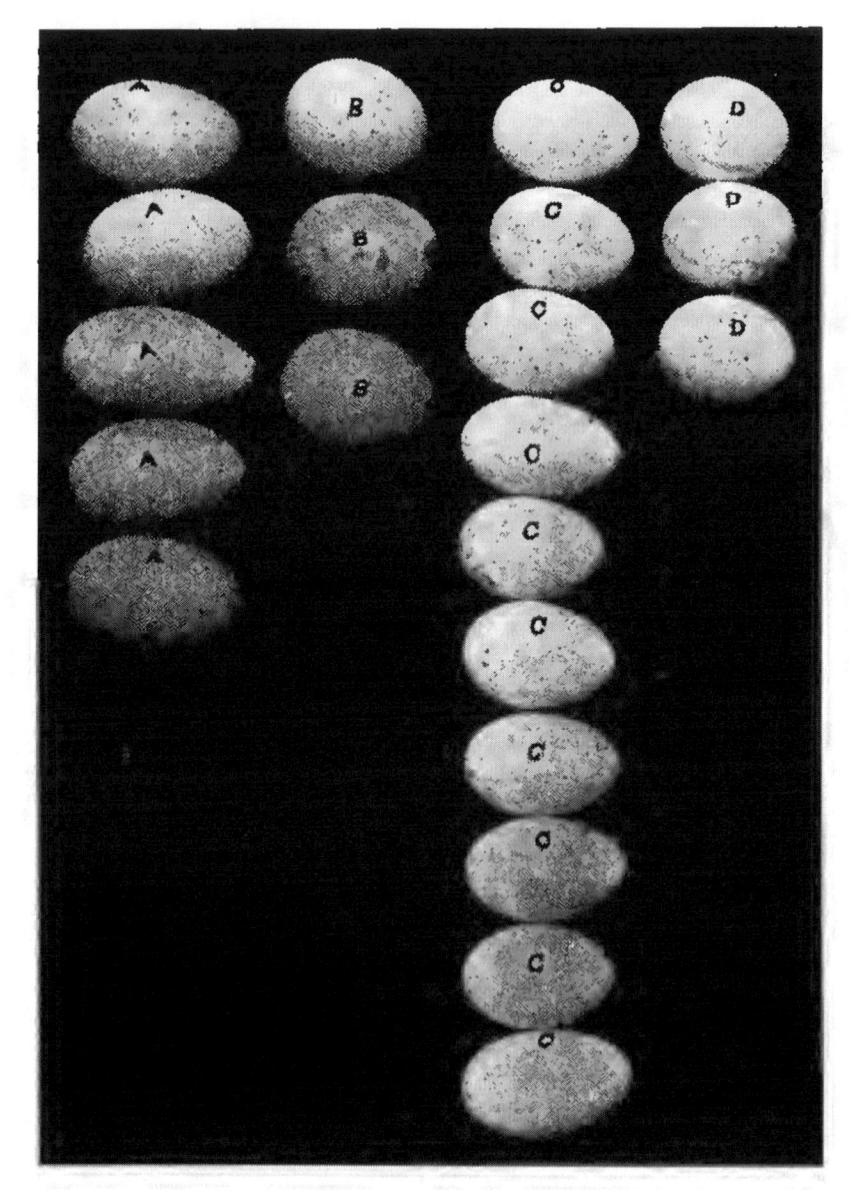

FIG. 10. FORMS OF EGGS.

characteristics distinguishing the egg were so marked that scarcely any error was made guessing the identity of the hen that laid them. The eggs marked (a) were distinguishable by their large size, extreme length and rich uniform light brown color; eggs marked (b) by their perfect egg shape, large size and dark brown color; eggs marked (c) by their long, thin form with a tendency to a slight ridge in the center; eggs marked (d) by their almost abnormal roundness; eggs marked (e) by the peculiar wart-like excrescence on the small end of each egg.

Abnormal eggs are due either to injury to the fowl while the egg is being formed or to faulty nutrition. The cuts represent various types of abnormal eggs. (a) and (l) are too long; (m), (e) and (o) too round; (k) is wedge shaped; (o) has a decided ridge at the center; (f) and (q) are flattened on one side; those marked (j) are elliptical; (i)

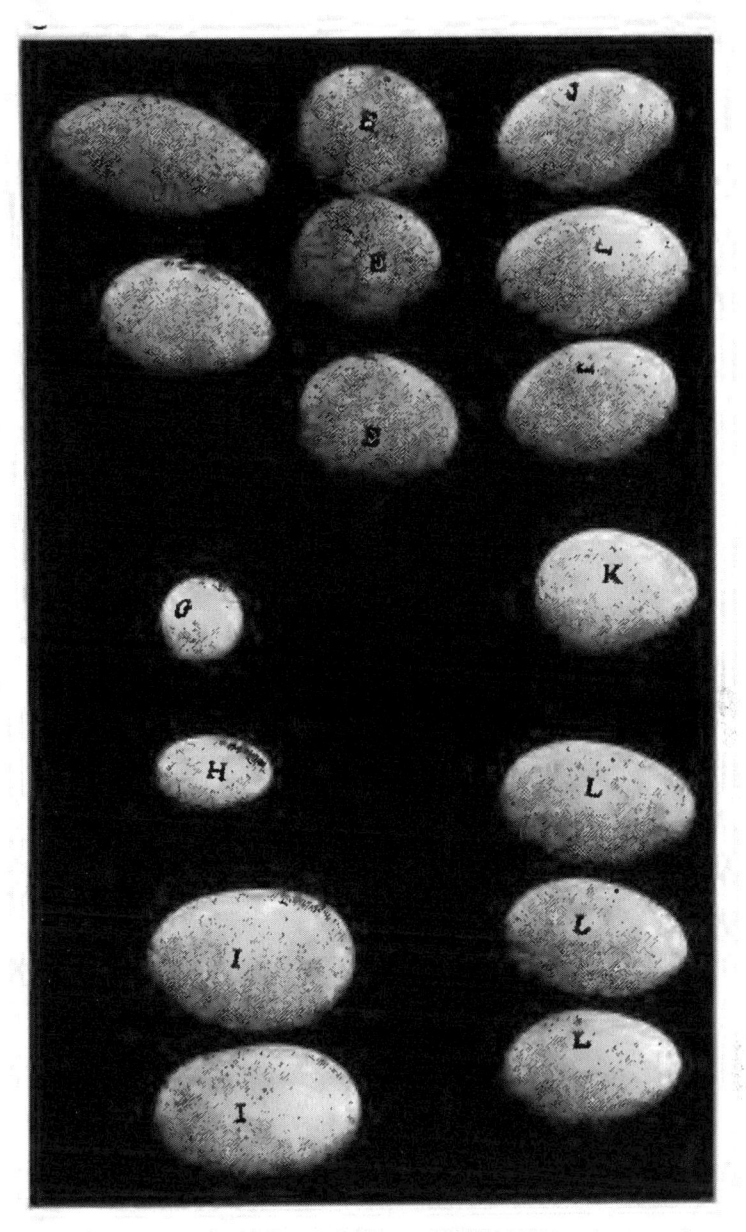

FIG. 11. FORMS OF EGGS.

are almost cylindrical; (a) is drawn out at the point; (p) are eggs with rough, weak shells; (g) is as round as a marble and about the size of a hickorynut; (h) is about the same size, but elongated; those marked (r) represent the two extremes, a double-yolked egg and a diminutive but perfect shaped egg. These small eggs are nearly always devoid of yolks. It does not follow that a hen that lays a diminutive egg has laid similar eggs previously or that she will do so again. Eggs marked (g) were all laid by the Single Comb White Leghorn hen No. 85; those marked (h) were laid by the Single Comb White Leghorn hen No. 82, the two normal eggs in each case being laid a few days after the abnormal. The abnormality, however, may continue. One hen laid seven diminutive eggs continuously and then stopped laying. Of the five eggs marked (a), Fig. 10, the first two eggs which are perfect and normal were followed by the abnormal long-drawn-out egg which was so weak at the point that it scarcely retained the egg contents. Within two or three days following the other two eggs were laid which were perfectly normal and sound.

Just how long it takes for each part of the egg to be secreted is not known. The whole process is supposed to take about 18 hours. Considerable time is taken for the shell to be deposited and to harden. Two eggs can be under way at the same time. When the hen is not laying the oviduct is shrunken and not more than one-fifth its natural size. Like all secretory glands, the oviduct enlarges with the activity of the organ. In this one respect it may be compared with the udder of a cow "fresh in milk" and one "gone dry." The oviduct when stretched out and congested is normally a little over 20 inches long.

The development of an egg is more elaborate and more exhaustive than a simple secretion like that of milk-making. It is both a reproductive and a secretory process. The perfect egg contains the materials and the life to form a new animal, a shell to protect it during subsequent development, and the food to nourish it for several days after it is born. A good hen is expected to lay, that is, to give birth to, about 150 offspring in a year, which is equivalent to about five times her own weight. This is a heavy drain upon her system. Something of its immediate effect will be seen by the fact ascertained by one of our students (Henry Jennings) that a hen's temperature immediately after laying is from two to three degrees higher than normal, the normal being about 106.

The composition of the egg remains practically constant. This is true even under different systems of feeding. Careful observation of two pens of Plymouth Rock hens was made and the eggs analyzed after they had been fed about three months on radically different rations. Pen one was fed largely on protein-rich foods; pen two was fed largely on foods deficient in protein, the former being a ration for making muscle and the latter for making fat. Nevertheless the eggs from the two pens remained practically identical in composition. This illustrates one of the highest laws of nature, namely, that the animal will sacrifice its own bodily strength in order to make a perfect offspring, which is a necessary provision to insure the perpetuation of the species. There is little difference in the composition of eggs from different breeds, or between light-shelled and dark-shelled eggs.

There is a difference between hens that are well fed and those that are improperly fed, as shown in their fertility, the strength of the germs and the vitality of the chickens. The chemist may not be able to find it in the composition, but the difference is there nevertheless. Hens that are closely confined to limited quarters where they do not get exercise nor have access to sunshine and fresh air, even though well fed, are almost certain to produce eggs low in fertility and weak in vitality. Over-fat hens and very poor hens, if they lay at all, are certain to produce eggs which are almost devoid of the life-giving principles.

While forced feeding of highly stimulating foods during Fall and Winter might result in a condition of nerve exhaustion during the hatching season and would naturally result in less fertile eggs, it does not follow that just because hens do not lay during Fall and Winter that they will give more fertile eggs during the Spring. Most frequently the hens that do not lay during the Winter have not been properly cared for, they being either too fat from over-feeding or improper feeding, or too poor because underfed. The fowl that lays the most fertile eggs is the one that is in the best health. She may be the hen that has laid regularly for a long period of time. To get fertile eggs, open-air exercise and plenty of meat and green food are necessary.

The proportion of males to females in the breeding of flock depends upon the breed, also upon the individual. One vigorous, active, prepotent male will give greater fertility than three or four sluggish, effeminate males. I have known almost perfect fertility with 36 White Leghorn females to one male, and have seen almost absolute infertility where one male ran with 15 females. Other conditions being equal, the Mediterranean, Leghorns, Minorcas, etc., class can usually be mated 20 to 25 females to one male; the American class (Plymouth Rocks, Wyandottes, Javas, etc.) 15 to 20 females to one male; Asiatic (Cochins, Brahmas, etc.) 10 to 15 females to one male. Where fowls are kept in flocks which require two males (for instance, 40 or 50 Leghorn females,) it is better to allow only one of the males at a time with the flock. The other one should be kept in a coop with plenty of water, grit and food containing an abundance of meat. Two males running together in the same flock dissipate too much of their energy in fighting. This is particularly true if they are in limited quarters. Very good results, however, are obtained by allowing one male to 25 females where fowls run together in flocks of several hundred on unlimited range.

The shape, size and color of the egg being comparatively constant with individuals, it is evident that like other characteristics they can be transmitted from one generation to another, and therefore by selecting only eggs of a certain size, shape and color for hatching, their characteristics become fixed so that a strain of hens will be developed which will lay eggs of the desired type with great regularity. This has been demonstrated in my own experience, where for years we have used only eggs that weigh two ounces or more, of perfect shape, pure white color, for hatching.

Each year the percentage of hatchable eggs has astonishingly increased, and the number of eggs which would have to be thrown out because of not fulfilling the requirements has materially decreased. The result is that the average size and beauty of the egg has materially increased year by year. This principle was strikingly illustrated during my boyhood days on the old farm, where my aunt, who took charge of the hens believed that round eggs would hatch pullets and long eggs slightly wrinkled at the small end would hatch cockerels. For years she would select the roundest eggs for hatching, with the result that year by year our eggs became rounder and rounder, until they were abnormally so, and it became almost a trade mark of the eggs from my grandfather's farm. Of course the per cent of pullets continued as usual. Wise Mother Nature could not be thwarted so easily. The sex of an egg cannot be determined by its shape or by any other external conditions.

It is well to select only perfectly shaped eggs, uniform in color, of good texture and firm shell, neither over large nor very small, because they will be more apt to produce chickens that lay similar eggs, which look better, and therefore sell for a higher price, and which also hatch more satisfactorily. Eggs which differ in size get different degrees of heat in the incubators, because the larger the egg the warmer it will become, it being closer the source of heat above. The more uniform eggs are in texture of shell the more uniformly they evaporate moisture. Eggs, like milk, being a direct secretion of the blood, are affected in color, flavor and odor by the foods consumed.

Keeping eggs weakens their vitality. If they are held at too low a temperature the chilling injures them. If they are kept in too warm a temperature, development begins. Just what temperature is best for holding eggs for hatching is not known. It appears to be between 55 and 65 degrees Fahrenheit. Eggs evaporate moisture very rapidly if kept in a very dry room. Therefore they should be kept from a direct draft of air. They should be turned daily in order to prevent the yolks rising to the surface and adhering to the shell, in which case the vitelline membrane may become ruptured when the egg is turned. Eggs should prove fertile within three or four days after the male has been introduced to the flock. They should be fertile with the second egg after copulation takes place and may be fertile with the first egg.

CHAPTER V.

Hatching the Egg.

WHAT IS INCUBATION?—A barnyard hen of the larger breeds will, if left to herself with enough food, "steal her nest." She finds some secluded place, makes a shallow hole and lays a clutch of eggs in it. She then sits on the eggs, leaving them at intervals for water and food and to dust herself, until they are hatched. It is sometimes asked why such a hen, operating in this crude way, will hatch more and stronger chicks than an incubator, or than most hens when put on selected eggs in a comfortable nest. The chicks from the stolen nest are generally uniform because they are likely to be all from one hen; thus they are sure to be much alike, and more likely to be fertile than when picked from a flock. They are strong because the hen works for her food, roaming about the farm picking up a variety, and exercising so as not to be too fat or dumpy. Left to herself, too, the hen lays eggs in her stolen nest just when they are most likely to be suitable for hatching. Thus she sets an example in feeding, selection and breeding. In trying to breed improved stock man attempts to imitate the barnyard hen, and at the same time increase the number of her eggs and make sure of her mating. In the same way when we build an incubator we try to imitate the hen by putting the eggs in a box in a chamber where they may be surrounded by the conditions of heat and moisture which the hen puts around her eggs in the nest.

A broody hen is fat. The organ of incubation is developed. This organ is a network of veins on the lower part of the hen's body. At the time of hatching, that is, when the hen becomes "broody," these veins enlarge and carry more blood, so that a warmer surface is presented to the eggs than would be the case if the hen were not broody. The hen's feathers permit a slight circulation of air to the eggs, and some little moisture comes from her body. The hen leaves her nest at times, or stands up and shakes herself, thus cooling the eggs. She also moves the eggs about from time to time. It is a question whether the hen does this because she knows it is necessary, or because she tries to arrange the eggs so as to make the nest most comfortable. In artificial incubation it has been found best to turn the eggs frequently, the chief reason given for doing so being that if the eggs are not turned the germs may dry fast to the shells early in the hatch.

In artificial incubation we attempt to surround the eggs with temperature and moisture such as the hen gives them from her body. Under the influence of a steady, gentle heat the life in the egg develops rapidly and in perfect order. An incubator cannot think, and the best of man's thoughts can hardly equal the instinct of the hen. Yet after long experience and observation a poultryman comes to acquire an instinct nearly equal to that of the hen. We do not attempt to give here a scientific essay on incubation. A few practical rules follow, but we know from experience that this is one of the operations that a man must grow into by his own study and practice. Some natural mechanics have made incubators of their own which give fair satisfaction, but our advice is to buy a good one rather than to tinker with a home-made affair. There is no other machine now offered for sale which is so fully explained in the catalogues of manufacturers, and one can hardly go wrong if he will follow the advice given him there. It is a wise plan, when starting with an incubator, to set a hen and compare the eggs under her with those in the incubator. Where this is done day by day we get a clearer idea of the way our incubator eggs should "test." While an egg can be tested by an expert by holding it up in a dark room before a light, it is better for the beginner to obtain a "tester" made for the purpose. As all know, the egg is tested by holding it, surrounded by a dark background, before a flame, so that the light will shine through it. The light of the candle or lamp reveals to us, in the egg, what the X-Ray does in the human body!

HATCHING UNDER HENS.—There are many poultrymen who depend upon hens to hatch most of their chicks, in spite of the ease with which incubators are handled. When given a fair chance the hen does not need regulating. The hens of the larger breeds lay their clutch of eggs and then show by their actions that they are ready to sit. Everyone who has handled hens knows how they act when broody. They get on the nest, ruffle up their feathers, come as near as they can to growling when approached, and strike with their bills. The whole nature of the hen changes, and if she be given a comfortable nest with the eggs that she can cover with her body she will usually stay by them until they are hatched. Mr. Cosgrove, of Connecticut, gives the following account of his method of handling sitting hens:

"I have a little house 6 x 10 feet, with two rows of nests, one row above the other; the ground forms the bottom of the lower nests, and in the upper ones I put a large shovelful of sifted earth, pushing it up into the corners so as to make it concave enough to keep the eggs together, but not too much so. If the center is an inch lower than the outside edge, it is sufficient. A board six inches wide by 10 feet long forms the front of the nests, so the hens can step into them; they do not have to jump down on to the eggs.

"The earth floor of the house dug up, and the stones taken out, makes the best dust bath, and a feed trough and water pail are all the furniture required. I keep feed in the trough all the time, also some grit and oyster shells in one end of it. The trough is made with a cover to it so the hens can stick their heads in to eat, but cannot soil the food. Whole corn is the main feed, but I give some wheat with it once or twice a week for variety. Some people have a great deal of trouble to make hens sit in any place except where they have been laying, but if the change of place is done rightly there is seldom any difficulty.

"Don't move them in the daytime. Don't take them by the legs and carry them along with heads handing down and thrust them in on the nests, as I have seen folks do—carrying three in each hand—and then expect them to stay put.

"I save the unhatched eggs from my incubators to put in nests to try the hens on. Let the hen sit at least two days on her own nest before you move her where you want her to sit; then after dark take the hen and put her gently on the eggs. She will usually settle down on them at once and stay on all night, but may come off in the morning and stay off all day, but will generally go on the nest at night, and then it is safe to put the good eggs under. If she does not go back on the nest at night, it is no use trying that hen any further. It doesn't pay to try to confine the hen on the nest; a hen is feminine, and if she won't, *she won't*.

"My sitting house has three windows facing the nests, which make it too light, so I tack grain bags over the windows, as hens like a secluded place better. I give all sitting hens a thorough dusting with insect powder and scatter some in the nests before setting, and again about a week before they are due to hatch. When the hens are sitting it is necessary to look at them once or twice a day to see that all the nests have hens on, for sometimes two get on the same nest, but don't be discouraged if the eggs are cold; they will usually hatch just as well; it will delay the hatch, that is all.

"Of course hens may be allowed to sit where they have been laying, by marking the eggs put under them, and removing the eggs laid to them every day, but there is considerable risk of broken eggs, also that the sitter may be driven off and go on some other nest. In some cases the nests in the 'sitting room' are made double; that is, they are deep, with a partition at the center. The eggs are put in the rear part. The hen may if she likes get off the nest and come in front. Thus a hen that is tired of sitting is less likely to break her eggs. The nests are sometimes closed with a gate, so that the hen is shut in, being let out once a day for a few minutes to eat and drink and dust."

Hens of the larger breeds will sometimes remain broody for three months. They will frequently hatch out two and three broods in succession—the chicks being taken away, and put in a brooder. Where a number of hens are set together it is a good plan to test the eggs as we do those in an incubator. By taking out the infertile eggs we can put what is left under part of the hens and start the others on a new lot.

BREAKING UP A BROODY HEN.—With the larger breeds the sitting hen becomes a nuisance in May or June. They often become broody too late in the season to rear chicks for Fall laying. To "break them up" we must remember that they are in a feverish condition, with the blood vessels on the lower part of the body enlarged. They must be "cooled off." Do not duck them in water or tie them by one leg or put them in a box with sharp spikes in the bottom. Make a "hen jail" at the side of the henhouse—raised above the floor. Have the bottom of slats, so that the air circulates under the hen. Put her there with water and grass, but no corn. She will soon find that there are no chickens to be hatched out of a slat, and she will keep off the nests where the other hens lay. This is far better than putting the hen in a yard with a young dog or a lively cockerel to chase her about. As the broody hen is fat do not feed her on the fattening foods.

ARTIFICIAL INCUBATION.—It is well to start the season's labors with a firm faith in our incubators, and that success or failure in results rests with ourselves.

1. The hens whose eggs we use for hatching should be healthy young fowls, and best returns are generally received where a single strain is employed. In a mixed lot the shells are of all grades in thickness; consequently some are apt to dry down too much, and others not enough. For example, the White Wyandotte eggs require much more ventilation than do White Leghorns.

2. The eggs should be set on the small end and turned half over every 24 hours. They should be placed in a cool, dry, clean, sweet-smelling room. Hens' eggs, if carefully looked after, will keep for hatching purposes three to four weeks. During the cool Spring days duck eggs, under same conditions, will keep 10 days to two weeks. When warm weather sets in they spoil very quickly; in from four days to a week's time.

As a rule incubators do best in a clean, well ventilated cellar, because the temperature is likely to run more even, thus giving the operator less trouble, and also because the atmosphere contains a moist, humid element, favorable to the growth and development of the chicks in embryo.

The instructions regarding setting up and operating, which accompany the incubator, cannot be too carefully studied and followed. There is usually, however, a clause concerning ventilation and moisture, which necessarily leaves much to the operator's good sense and judgment, because, owing to the difference in climatic conditions in our country, which tend to affect the results in artificial incubation, no cut and dried rule can be laid down or successfully applied.

Where these conditions are normal, general directions on these heads are all that the operator requires; but in low-lying sections and near lakes or large rivers, where fogs or humidity prevails, very little additional moisture, and considerable ventilation are necessary; while in a rarified atmosphere, elevated or mountainous localities, a very considerable amount of moisture is necessary to secure even a fair hatch, and not nearly so much ventilation. The tea kettle or the drying of the roads are good guides for evaporation and moisture. Also, in the same locality, there are times when a change of method is necessary, as in sustained droughts, when high, dry winds prevail, or during a long wet season, etc. If the machine is run in a living room, more moisture is needed, and in every case good care should be taken to keep the chicks well supplied with pure, fresh air, by ventilating the room thoroughly at least twice a day, night and morning, when the eggs are being turned. Kerosene odors and exhausted air are very injurious to the hatch.

From the above it will be seen that the climate and atmospheric conditions must be studied and the rig managed accordingly. If the chicks hatch small and look shrunken, and the inner skin sticks to some and outer skin is thick and leathery, they had insufficient moisture and too much ventilation. If they simply failed to break the shell, the birds were weakened by insufficient ventilation, and, perhaps, also, a wrong temperature. If the birds are surrounded—"swim"—in a gluey, watery substance, too much moisture was applied. If they come out ahead of time, the temperature was run too high; if they run over time, it was too low. If during the hatch, through accident, the thermometer registers high for several hours, the hatch will probably be hurried out a little, while if it is low, especially during the first five days, the hatch will drag along, even four days after due. It is best to hang on to the eggs until hope is utterly dead. A bath in tepid water helps such cases quite a bit, and those that "wiggle" are apt to come out; give them time, and with care they will develop usually into healthy chicks.

Regarding testing of eggs, and growth of air cells, dark-colored shells do not show fertility very plainly until the hatch is about half over. Usually in five days the germ is quite plain in white or thin-shelled eggs, but it is well to place the doubtful ones together and give them one more chance. About two days before exclusion at the final test, all that do not show full development should be discarded. A very little experience will enable the operator to detect the little black, spider-like form with red pulses, and the gradual darkening of the egg as development progresses; the clear beauty of the infertile egg, and wavy, watery, cloudy appearance of the bad one; the red ring or black splotch of the dead germ.

As regards the growth of the air cell, our experience is that no combination of circumstances, in our section, will coax them to enlarge in the regular fashion shown in books. With us, two-thirds of the drying down is done the last week. If everything has gone well, the eggs dry down during those last few days about right; if anything has gone wrong they show it then, either by drying down too much, or not enough. Therefore there is no need to worry about the air cell; it will take care of itself, and it cannot be used as a guide for the application of moisture or ventilation; as it opens up too late to be of any use to the operator. Also, if the chicks are vigorous, they will kick out of the shell with quite a small air space, while weak birds fail to escape from those that are dried down to "regulation."

It is best to trim and fill the lamps in the morning, and regulate the machine then, for the next 24 hours. Never touch the lamp at night. Turn the eggs early.

While chicks are usually all out of the shell 24 hours after the first pip is noticed, ducks require 48 hours to finish up in. We say "the hatch is over," and are ready to open and clean up when most of the birds that we see are fully out of the shell and dried off. If partially liberated birds that are sticking to the shell at some point can be found at just the right time—not too soon or too late—they can be saved. Just how much this sort of assistance pays it is difficult to say. The writer helped 22 ducklings out once, and tied a red string to the leg of each; and so far as one could keep track of the gang, they survived and throve with the best of the lot. It seems well therefore to give the little fellows any chance for life that we can, though undoubtedly the best way is to "get the right flop" on managing the incubator and let it do the hatching.

Just before "opening up" prepare everything for a quick shift—an assistant, pan of hot water, two flannel cloths, and let the temperature run up to 106 or 107. Take out a tray and clean off all but pipped eggs, and help the birds out, placing them on the wet flannel spread on the tray; add to them the same sort of eggs from the other tray. Promptly replace it in the incubator, and the other flannel steaming hot anywhere inside the rig. Get the temperature to 104½ degrees quickly as possible. A few hours more and the birds will probably all be liberated. If a chipped egg has a live chick in it, you can hear its bill tapping on the shell if you place it to your ear.

When eggs are shipped from a distance, if duck eggs, they cannot be got into the incubator or under the hen too soon. If hen or turkey eggs, they should be placed in a quiet, cool place till required, but 24 hours is long enough to hold them.

Though nearly all incubators on the market can be made to produce fair hatches, there is a great difference in the amount of time and care needed to secure them. This is due to the variety of contrivances employed to regulate the heat in the egg chamber. The incubator, therefore, of most value to the operator, is the one that has the most simply constructed, conservative and accurate regulator. There are machines that will hold the heat steady for nearly a week without the operator's help, and at considerable fluctuation in outside atmosphere. The need therefore for bobbing up and down nights to watch refractory hatches is practically past. If—through any accident—the heat runs up too high, when regulating it back to normal figures, it helps the eggs to cool with least injury, if they are well sprinkled with tepid water. The incubator doors can be left open till the thermometer registers 90 degrees. In all cases and at all times of handling them drafts should be avoided over the eggs, and sudden jars.

DEVELOPMENT OF THE CHICK.—We have seen that a fertile egg is not a shell packed with a loose and unorganized fluid. It contains definite organs and the material required to feed and develop them into a living chick. When the proper heat is applied in the incubator or under the hen life begins and develops rapidly until the last of the yolk in the egg is passed into the body of the well-formed chick before it leaves the shell. Before 12 hours of incubation the germ begins to increase in size, and so rapidly does the development go on that by the end of the first day what is to be the head of the chick can be quite plainly seen. A few hours later the tail of the chick is apparent, to be immediately followed by a tube which later forms the heart. About 40 hours after the incubation begins the heart begins to pulsate. The knowledge of this rapid development may not be cheerful reading to those who let the eggs in the nest remain for a day or two under a sitting hen, but by the fiftieth hour the heart is usually so well developed that the different parts may be seen, and 10 hours later a vigorous circulation of blood has begun. Before the third day has ended the rapidly forming chick is able to turn itself around and curve into definite shape. During the fourth day the limbs begin to show. They grow so rapidly that by the thirteenth day scales appear upon the legs and nails upon the toes, and by the sixteenth day these, as well as the beak become firm and hard and the chick can move its limbs. By the ninth day the formation of bone begins and goes on rapidly until the skeleton is well formed by the thirteenth day. The feathers begin as little sacs by the tenth day and develop so that when the chick makes its way through the shell it is well feathered. Thus this wonderful and rapid development goes on inside the egg. We must remember that the power of the delicate machinery which produces the chicks comes from its parents. They must be vigorous, well fed, not closely related, and able to exercise freely if we expect vigorous chicks. It may seem to the novice that the egg hatches itself since the hen is usually successful. He will change his views after trying to imitate her with an incubator, and also find that he must learn the hen business by experience.

CHAPTER VI.

The Chicken's Nurse.

The beginner with poultry is often discouraged over losses of little chicks. Where incubators are used, it is of course impossible to find hens to brood the chicks. Hens will sometimes "sit" long enough to hatch two broods. Thus several hens can be started at one time and the chicks put together in a brooder, more eggs being put under the hens. A brooder is a chicken nurse. In using it we try to confine warm air among pieces of soft cloth—in imitation of the hen's warm body and soft feathers.

There are many different kinds of brooders, the best of them so arranged that the warm air will come from above, just as the heat of the hen is above the chicks. This heat may come from hot water or steam pipes run above the chicks, or from kerosene lamps or gas burners below them, with the heat forced above. Unless one is a natural mechanic and handy with tools he should buy one of the readymade brooders. We would not advise one to try to make an incubator, though it has been done, but it is possible to make a brooder that will keep the chicks warm and provide them with fresh air. The homemade brooder pictured here is known as the "Cosgrove" and is described as follows. It will give an idea of the principles upon which a hot-air brooder is built.

HOMEMADE BROODER.—"The material required is an empty one-pound coffee can, a two-pound coffee can, a piece of galvanized sheet iron 24x36 inches, with a hole in center that will just fit the one-pound can, 85 feet of seven-eighths-inch matched pine and six feet of one-half-inch pine. Make the four sides of the box nine inches high; that will just take in the sheet iron; put strips ⅞x1 inch inside the box two inches below top edge, for the sheet iron to rest on. Take the one-pound can and cut slits a half inch apart all around the top edge; cut just down to where the bulge in the tin is (about one-half inch), put the slit part through the sheet iron and bend the slit pieces down flat on the iron. The bulge prevents the can from going through the iron, and if the slit pieces are hammered down tight it makes nearly an air-tight job, but to make sure that no fumes from the lamp get above the sheet iron it is better to solder it tight. Place the iron in the box

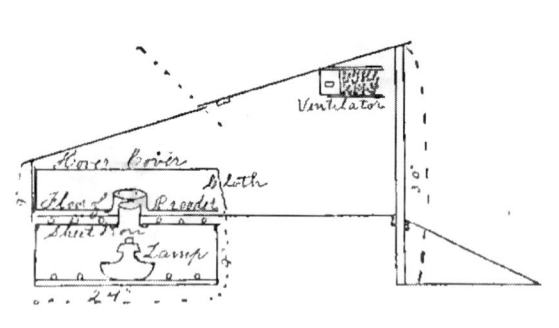

FIG. 12. HOMEMADE BROODER.

and nail strips on top of iron, pressing it down tight on the under strips. Nail a floor of 7/8-inch stuff on top of box, cutting a hole in center the size of the two-pound coffee can; slit the can like the other, bend the pieces out and nail on top of floor, but first punch the top of can full of one-fourth-inch holes to let the hot air out. Then bore five or six half-inch holes on the two ends through

FIG. 13.
VAN DRESSER BROODER HOUSE.

side of box between sheet iron and floor of brooder to let in air; also four holes in each end of box one inch in diameter near bottom edge to let in air for lamp. The rest is plain carpenter work. Take a piece nine inches wide, length of box and nail or screw on back end, letting it come down only an inch or so below the edge of box. Then nail on sides, using two 2 x 2-inch posts 30 inches long to hold up front end. I line the hover part with one-half-inch pine 6½ inches wide, nailing on strips at top and bottom edge one-half inch square, so that it makes a half-inch air space on ends and back.

"The hover cover of 7/8-inch stuff rests on this lining and is not fastened, can be lifted out to clean out brooder, and as chicks get old enough is removed entirely. To the front of hover cover are tacked strips of cloth two inches wide, reaching the floor. Some of these cloth strips can be turned up on top of cover to let out hot air on warm days. On front part of sides bore holes as shown in figure, and make a sliding cover so as to close or open these holes. The amount of air entering the half-inch holes above sheet iron and passing over chicks is governed by these ventilators. The front half of roof is screwed to sides and front and middle bar. The back half is loose and projects three inches under front part; can be lifted up as shown by dotted lines, then by lifting hover cover the floor can be easily cleaned.

"The lamps I use have no chimneys. Flame of lamp should be about two inches below level of sheet iron. Cut a hole in

FIG. 14.
COLD COUNTRY BROODER HOUSE.

FIG. 15.
MAPES' BROODER HOUSE.

back of box to enter lamp and have a sliding cover to it. If lamp flame burns dim make more holes in side of box, or open slide a little. Bore five or six half-inch holes in back of box three inches below sheet iron to let lamp fumes out, if there are any. The front, with the exception of a six or eight-inch piece nailed to posts at top, is an independent piece held in place by buttons, and comes out, so the whole interior can be got at. Make a frame to hold a glass, say 12 x 20 inches (the larger the better), bevel top and bottom edge of frame and nail beveled strips at top and bottom, so glass frame will slide to make a hole as large or small as you want to feed the chicks through. With lamp taking a wick only ⅝-inch wide I have had no difficulty in keeping heat in these brooders at 90 to 100 degrees."

BROODER HOUSES.—We do not attempt to give details for a brooder house. No one should try to build a house without visiting one in successful operation. The principle is a long, low house divided into pens, in each one of which is a brooder—that is, a warm box with hover cloths. These brooders are heated by lamps or by hot-water pipes which run through the house so as to pass through each brooder. Little runs protected by wire netting are made so that the chicks can run out on pleasant days. As the chicks grow larger they are taken from this large nursery and put outdoors. There is much argument between the advocates of the large brooder house and those who prefer what is called the colony plan. The large house is evidently better in very cold weather, and it is less work to care for a given number of chicks when they are all in one house. There is greater danger from fire, and also greater danger in case of disease among the flock. Those who use the colony plan build a small warm house with a single brooder inside. This is heated by a lamp or flame. Gasoline is now being successfully used for this purpose. From 50 to 200 little chicks are put in this house, and the heat kept up to a point that will make the entire house comfortable. The chicks run about in the house, and except in very cold days, do not crowd under the hover. On pleasant days they are let out and run on the grass. When heat is no longer needed, and the chicks grow large enough, the brooder is taken out and little roosts are put in so that the young birds early become used to a house. Fig. 13 shows such a house and brooder used by Henry Van Dresser, who uses these houses to scatter his chicks through the orchards. Fig. 14 shows a colony brooder house used at the Maine Experiment Station, where the Winters are very cold and the snow very deep. These houses, it must be remembered, have nothing inside but the brooders. Fig. 15 shows a house used by O. W. Mapes, and Fig. 16 a house used for young White Leghorns in New Jersey. These houses are designed for sheltering the chicks when they are taken from the large brooder house. They contain a brooder at first, but as the chicks grow larger roosts are put in. The object in arranging these houses is to give the pullets a place where they may have heat if needed, and at the same time become used to living in a house, while having plenty of exercise. As we shall see, the best breeders separate the young roosters early and put them by themselves. It is absolutely necessary that these brooders and brooder houses be *kept clean*. Dirt and vermin are far more fatal to little chicks than to grown-up hens.

FIG. 16. NEW JERSEY BROODER HOUSE.

We must remember that what is clean to one man may be filthy to another. The little chicks are weak and unable to care for themselves when they are put in the brooder. Vermin and disease live in filth and we cannot be too careful about cleaning the brooders before a new lot of chicks are put in. The brooder should be made so that it opens readily. When a brood has grown so that the chicks can be taken away the brooder should be opened and thoroughly scrubbed out with hot water. The corners should be smeared with kerosene and the hover taken out and carefully gone over. The brooder should, if possible, stand open to the sun in order to dry thoroughly before the new chicks are put in. These things are emphasized by those who discuss the care of the little chicks, but they cannot be made too plain. Those who have seen little chicks suffer from damp brooders or seen them suffocated by lamp fumes or chilled when the lamp burns too low, or wasted when it goes too high, know the necessity of using a competent chicken nurse.

CHAPTER VII.

Care of the Baby Chick.

Neither brooder nor incubator can think. Both require constant attention, or the eggs or chicks may be too hot or too cold. The old hen looks after her brood, and sees that they are made comfortable. Man must be half hen, and let his brooder represent the other half. Even when the hen hatches the chicks she cannot be expected to nurse them as a cow would nurse a calf! If it is possible to give it the chicks will do better with a free range with hen, but hawks, rats and other vermin may get too many of the little ones. If these pests are bad the hen may be kept in a coop and a frame made for the chicks by placing four 12-inch-wide boards on edge with inch-mesh wire netting over the entire top. This gives the chicks a run and protects them. Even when free range is possible the hen should not be given entire charge until the chicks are strong enough to follow without being tired out. Do not think the hen can scratch a living for a large family out of the dirt. Give hen and chicks when at large at least two feeds a day of grain. The following account of the care given the hen and her chicks is given by a successful poultry keeper:

HENS AND LITTLE CHICKS.—"My little 'setting' house has nests for 16 hens, and I try to set as many at a time as I can. When the chicks are hatched I take them all out of the nests, put them in a big market basket with a warm woollen cloth to cover them, then selecting the hens that seem the most anxious about their chicks (for the mother instinct varies as much in hens as in human beings, some even picking and killing their chicks as fast as hatched) I put the hens in little "A" coops (see **Fig. 17**) made with the slats perpendicular, the back boarded up, the upper half of back hinged to lower half and held in place by button at top. Made in this way the hen can be got at easily, or a dead chick taken out of the coop without difficulty, and on a cold windy day the wind does not sweep through coop, chilling the chickens, as it does when both ends of the coop are slatted.

"I place two of these coops about 10 feet apart, and connect them by two frames, one covered with inch-mesh wire netting for front, and back frame covered with half-inch matched boards, with a door at each end, so as to get at the front of the coops with feed and water. As the top part of the front frame is made of a board a foot wide, thus more than half of the runway is kept dry, and the chicks can run around on a rainy day without getting wet, and are safe from hawks and 'varmints.' As these frames are only fastened to the coops by a nail or screw, they can be taken off and stored away in a shed in the Fall. When chicks are hatched in cold weather I put only 15 with each hen; in May or last of April I put 20 to 25 with each hen.

FIG. 17. HANDY HEN COOP.

"As the chicks are all the same color and age, the hens do not know their own chicks, and will take any of them. The chicks remain with the hen as long as she will mother them. Sometimes a hen will pick at the chicks and drive them away, as soon as she wants to lay eggs again; others will go to laying and continue to brood the chicks. I let them remain with the chicks as long as they will, until it becomes very hot weather; then I think the chicks are better off without the hen's heat. I feed and water them three times a day, and as soon as the cockerels weight two pounds each, send them to the market for broilers, reserving all the pullets for layers.

"The most dangerous enemy of chicks in this locality is the little Pigeon hawk, but in June they do not come around so frequently, and then I give the chicks the run of the farm. While they are confined green food is an absolute necessity if they are to thrive well, and lawn clippings furnish this in the best form, especially if cut in the early morning while the dew is still on the grass; I tie a box behind the lawn mower and the clippings fly into it, so it is no trouble to collect them. Insect powder sprinkled on the hen and in the nest freely a week before hatching usually drives away all lice. In hot weather, if the chicks and hens run together, the chicks will get lousy; then I put some of the powder mixed with lard on their heads, if they have head lice, and sprinkle it on their bodies if they have body lice, which are very different things. Two or three times in tne Summer I whitewash the coops with some crude carbolic acid in the whitewash; this is a good disinfectant as well as insecticide. Roosters and pullets all run together until the males begin to pester the females, then they are separated and the roosters confined, the pullets running at large until snow drives them into confinement.

THE BROODER CHICK.—"With the first pipping of an egg in my incubator I start the lamps under the brooders, that they may be warmed up and regulated to 90 degrees before the chicks are ready to be put in. The chicks are left in the incubators for 30 to 36 hours after hatching. I cover the floors of brooders with sifted sand half an inch deep, laying in a supply in the Summer for that special use. Taking the chicks to the brooder house in a big market basket with a warmed woollen cloth over

FIG. 18. UNFINISHED HEN COOP.

them I take out the front of brooder and put the chicks in, and now they have their first feed of hard-boiled eggs, chopped very fine and purposely scattered on the clean sand, so that the chicks will get some grit in their gizzards with their first meal. Some so-called experts do not favor hard-boiled egg, but my experience is that chicks will eat it in preference to anything else than can be set before them. I always save all the infertile eggs for that use.

"With the first little 'cheep' that shows they are getting too cool I take a board half an inch shorter than inside width of brooder, and press the chicks all back through the cloth strips into the hover, leaving the board leaning against hover to prevent chicks getting out. This board is one and a half or two inches narrower than the height of hover, so that by turning up two or three of the cloth strips there will be sufficient ventilation. A better scheme would be to make a frame and cover it with fine netting to keep the chicks in. I feed the first two or three days about once in three hours, the third day making the feed half rolled oats (the common oatmeal) and half boiled egg, chopped together. The chicks will pick out all the egg first, but if you do not overfeed will eat the oatmeal too. To have the chicks continue to thrive, overfeeding must be avoided until they are five or six weeks old. After they are a week old we bake a cake of wheat bran and cornmeal, with a teaspoonful of baking powder to make it light, and feed fine cracked corn also. As soon as frost gets out of the ground and worms come up, I make it a point to dig some worms nearly every day for them. It is *live* food, and the tenderest meat to be got, but the chicks will be made sick if too many are fed. Green food of some kind is almost a necessity after they are three weeks old. I put a cabbage head in their yards, and they will eat it clear to the stump.

"In from three to five days, according to the weather, I let them out of the brooder, and begin educating them to go up the incline and into their hover when cool. Some will huddle into a corner and get chilled unless watched and pushed in. After four or five weeks they ought to be left outdoors, if the ground is bare. I have seen chickens in a neighbor's $300 brooder house gets pale and so weak they could not stand up, until he put brooders and all outdoors on the grass, and in less than a week they were all right. I make a cheap drinking fountain by cutting slits in a tin can half an inch apart, bending in the slit part, filling the can with water and placing on top of it the cover of a larger can, then by inverting the two you have a self feeding fountain that the chicks cannot get wet in, and that it may not get upset put a stone on top of the can, for dampness in a brooder is to be most carefully avoided. My brooders are cleaned out twice a week, all the sand scraped out; then with a fine sieve sift out all the droppings and spread the sand around again. If it is clean sand, not earth, it may be used many times."

ANOTHER METHOD.—At the Maine Experiment Station the following plan is carried out:—

"We make bread by mixing three parts cornmeal, one part wheat bran, and one part wheat middlings or flour, with skim-milk or water, mixing it very dry, and salting as usual for bread. It is baked thoroughly, and when well done if it is not dry enough so as to crumble, it is broken up and dried out in the oven and then ground in a mortar or mill. The infertile eggs are hard boiled and ground, shell and all, in a sausage mill. About one part of ground egg and four parts of bread crumbs are rubbed together until the egg is well divided. This bread makes up about one-half of the food of the chicks until they are five or six weeks old. Eggs are always used with it for the first one or two weeks, and then fine sifted beef scrap is mixed with the bread.

"When the chicks are first brought to the brooders, bread crumbs are sprinkled on the floor of the brooder among the grit, and in this way they learn to eat, taking in grit and food at the same time. After the first day the food is given in tin plates, four to each brooder. The plates have low edges, and the chicks go on to them and find the food readily. After they have had the food before them for five minutes the plates are removed. As they have not spilled much of it, they have little left to lunch on except what they scratch for. In the course of a few days light wooden troughs are substituted for the plates. The bottom of the trough is a strip of half-inch board, two feet long and three inches wide. Laths are nailed around the edges. The birds are fed four times a day in these troughs until they outgrow them, as follows: Bread and egg or scrap early in the morning; at half past nine o'clock dry grain, either pin-head oats, crushed wheat, millet seed or cracked corn. At one o'clock dry grain again, and the last feed of the day is of the bread with egg or scrap. Between the four feeds in the pans or troughs, millet seed, pin-head oats and fine cracked corn and later whole wheat, are scattered in the chaff on the floor for the chicks to scratch for. This makes them exercise, and care is taken that they do not find the food too easily.

"One condition is made imperative in our feeding. The food is never to remain in the troughs more than five minutes before the troughs are cleaned or removed. This insures sharp appetites at meal time, and guards against inactivity which comes from overfeeding. Charcoal, granulated bone, oyster shell and sharp grit are always kept by them, as well as clean water. Mangels are cut in slices, which they soon learn to pick. When the grass begins to grow they are able to get green foods from the yards. If the small yards are worn out before they move to the range, green cut clover or rape is fed to them. After the chickens are moved to the range they are fed in the same manner, except that the morning and evening feed is made of corn meal, middlings and wheat bran, to which one-tenth as much beef scrap is added. The other two feeds are of wheat and cracked corn. One year we fed double the amount of scrap all through the growing season, and had the April and May pullets well developed and laying through September and October. To our sorrow they nearly all moulted in December, so that month and next were nearly bare of eggs."

Still another simple method of feeding little chicks is thus described by O. W. Mapes:

"Our hatch of chicks is doing very nicely on nothing but ordinary oat flakes, with water to drink. They are now a week old, and the mash balanced ration will be substituted for the oat flakes during the next week. We got 240 chicks from this hatch, with five more that had to be helped out of the shell; 241 of these are still lively and bright at the end of the first week. Not a bad showing for the oat flakes, which are very handy to feed. This hatch was from 360 eggs, nearly 300 of which proved to be fertile. The incubator door was closed when eggs first began to pip, and not opened for 48 hours; 240 lively chickens were then removed and five more were helped from the shells. They were all placed in two brooders, given grit and water at once, and a few oat flakes scattered in the sand on the brooder floor. They ate but little the first day, but on the second day and since they have been ravenously hungry four or five times a day. I have tried to give just what they would clean up in four or five minutes. Some days they have been fed five times and others only four. There is still little left of the 10-pound bag from which the 240 have been fed the first week of their lives. A good rule is to begin at 7 A. M. and feed regularly every two and a half hours until 6 P. M. for the first two weeks. After that they can soon be reduced to three meals a day."

CHAPTER VIII.

The Young Bird.

THE YOUNG HEN.—When the hen deserts her chicks, or when the little things leave the brooders, the real business of their life begins. The object is to push the young pullet rapidly so as to have her laying as early as possible. It is best to give the pullets free range if possible— the exercise develops them, and they do well to hunt part of their food. An orchard with reasonably low trees is a good place for pullets. They will do little harm, and benefit themselves if they can roost in the trees during the Summer and early Fall. They should be fed an abundance of about the same food that gives best results with laying hens. As the nights grow cool the pullets should be put in the houses they are to live in through the Winter. Where pullets run at large and roost in trees it is hard to break the tree habit. They must be taught to come into an enclosure of some sort. We can throw the evening feed inside the house and shut the door while the pullets are inside eating their supper. If given a small yard one wing may be clipped. It is an advantage to get the pullets into Winter quarters early. It is a great change from their life of freedom, and they will require considerable time to settle down into business. They should not, of course, be permitted to roost in trees or without shelter during the cold storms of Fall. Before being housed for the Winter the pullets should be dusted with insect powder and the houses should be thoroughly cleaned. If we put vermin in with the pullets we can hardly expect to get rid of it through the Winter. We must depend on the pullets for our earliest eggs. The older hens moult during the late Summer and Fall, and do not lay until they have recovered from this change. It is therefore necessary to force the pullets steadily, so that they may be ready for laying as early as possible. The age at which pullets will begin to lay varies with the breed, and depends much upon the care and feeding. Instances are on record where Leghorns have begun to lay at less than 120 days old, but this is exceptional. In good weather chicks are weaned at from seven to 10 weeks old, and then run until late September or October. We want a steady, rapid growth on the pullet if we expect them to pay for their board in November and December. In order to have pullets laying by November 1st they must be hatched by the middle of April and pushed forward without stoppage. If they can be made to begin at this time they have a full year for laying, while if they do not start until January the pullets lose two of the most profitable months. The theory that if a pullet does not lay at her best during her first year, she will make up for it the next year, does not work out in practice. She should be started early and kept at it.

A hard test for a new beginner with poultry will often come in the Fall when the pullets demand careful and heavy feeding and yet do not lay an egg. They must be fed heavily with a fair amount of meat if we expect them to lay early, and it often seems like money thrown away when grain is high and funds are short. It is a good time to dispose of old hens and surplus roosters while the pullets are "eating their heads off," for the income from these sources helps pay the grain bill.

THE YOUNG COCKEREL.—In many flocks the young males are permitted to become a nuisance. They often run at large until Thanksgiving, eating large quantities of grain, so that when they are finally killed they have cost about all they bring. It is well understood that pigs or cattle make their cheapest gain while young. We have found the cost of producing a pound of pork on a pig weighing 125 pounds considerably less than on the same pig when it is fed to 250 pounds. The same is true of the young roosters in the average flock. The following plan of feeding is followed at the Maine Experiment Station, and is much better than the old method of letting the young birds run at large.

"When the chickens are moved to the field the sexes are separated. The cockerels are confined in yards, in lots of about 100, and fed twice daily on porridge made of four parts of cornmeal, two parts middlings or flour, and one part fine beef scrap. The mixed meals are wet with skim-milk or water—milk is preferred—until the mixture will just run, but not drop from the end of a wooden spoon. They are given what they will eat of this in the morning and again towards evening. It is left before them until all have eaten heartily, not more than hour at one time, after which the troughs are removed and cleaned. The cockerels are given plenty of shade and kept as quiet as possible.

"We have found our chickens that are about 100 days old at the beginning to gain in four weeks' feeding, from 1¾ to 2¼ pounds each and sometimes more. Confined and fed in this way they are meaty and soft, and in very much better market condition than though they had been fed generously on dry grains and given more liberty. Poultry raisers cannot afford to sell the chickens as they run, but they can profit greatly by fleshing and fattening them as described. Many careful tests in chicken feeding have shown that as great gains are as cheaply and more easily made, when the chickens, in lots not to exceed 100, are put in a house with a floor space of 75 to 100 feet and a yard of corresponding size, as when they are divided into lots of four birds each and confined in latticed coops, just large enough to hold them. Four weeks has been about the limit of profitable feeding, both in the large and small lots. Chickens gain faster while young. In every case birds that were 150 to 175 days old have given us comparatively small gains. The practice of successful poultrymen in selling the cockerels at the earliest marketable age is well founded, for chickens, sold at Thanksgiving are expensive products."

Of course if the cockerel is to be kept for breeding purposes he should not be handled in this way, or he would be of little use as a breeder. In that case he should be fed like the pullets and have a good range, so that he can pick up frame and vigor instead of fat. We can never obtain strong and profitable laying stock by breeding from fat and sluggish parents.

Experiments with young birds kept in small coops compared with a large flock kept in one house, with a suitable yard, show that the latter method pays better. The birds make a slightly larger gain, and there is less work in caring for them. Where skim-milk can be had it is very profitable for mixing the mash for the young roosters. The addition of meat meal or beef scrap to the cornmeal increases the gain. One of the most important things is to begin fattening while the birds are young. It was found that when young roosters, 170 days old, were started at fattening over eight pounds of grain mash were required to make one pound of live chicken. With similar birds, 95 days old, fed in the same way, less than six pounds of grain were needed for one pound of live gain.

THE BROILER.—We must repeat the caution about putting either cockerels or pullets into filthy houses. No bird can possibly put on flesh while covered with vermin. When fattened as described the young rooster makes a fine broiler. Formerly a larger bird was required for this trade, but of late years a smaller carcass has found a market and is in demand. These are called "squab broilers." Small breeds like the Leghorns make excellent broilers when penned and fed on soft food as described above. The experience of O. W. Mapes in developing this trade will help many who wish to make the best use of the young roosters. The average young rooster sold alive at Thanksgiving rarely nets the grower over 30 cents. We may fatten them so that they will bring far more than this, and save at least two months of feeding.

"It is quite a tedious job to pick 50 broilers nicely, without tearing the skin. In picking squab broilers it is more difficult still. I stepped into a store in New York, a couple of years ago, where game and poultry are made a specialty, to look at some squab broilers I saw hanging in the window. The proprietor told me that all his poultry must be dry picked, as the eye of his customers had to be pleased as well as the palate. This was in December, and I happened to have a lot of chicks at home about the right size. He named a price per pair, which amounted to about 60 cents per pound, if I would dress them as nicely as the ones he showed me. One of our local butchers pretends to be an expert, having worked at it in the West, and he promised to help me out. I took him down a few, but he tore them so badly that he soon gave up in disgust. Nothing daunted, I took them home again, and we pegged away at it ourselves. If those who are looking for profitable employment in Winter for farm help can succeed in raising a lot of broilers to be picked in Winter, there will be no lack of employment. We do not pretend to know how to do it quickly yet, but we can do it nicely, and sell them for top quotations or more. We are open for suggestions from those who know how to do it quickly. The first thing, of course, is to have good plump birds. They should have yellow skin and legs. Deprive them of food at least 12 hours before killing, so that the crop will be empty. Hang the birds up by both feet, and bleed by opening mouth and cutting main artery of neck, at base of tongue. It is important to draw all the blood, or it may settle under the skin where each feather is pulled, discoloring the skin. Pull large wing and tail feathers first, then smaller feathers, and finally the pin feathers. There are spots on each wing and on the breast, where the skin tears very easily. Great care must be exercised at these points. Aside from this, it seems to be simply a case where nimble fingers count. Our best pickers still require from 15 to 18 minutes for either a squab broiler or a two-pound broiler. Immerse in ice water just as quickly as feathers can be removed. This removes animal heat quickly and prevents discoloration of the abdomen. When ready for shipment, remove from ice water, and pack in pounded ice. We wrap the heads of our S. C. White Leghorn cockerels in a neat paper before packing. This adds to the attractive appearance of the shipment. The squab broilers should weigh 12 to 14 ounces each. They are used by the wealthy buyers, and demanded just at the time when they are hardest to produce. If eggs that are laid in November and December can be successfully converted into chickens, they are sure to sell for big prices."

CHAPTER IX.

The Hen's House.

Men build various kinds of houses for their own use. Some are convenient and comfortable; others are never satisfactory. If we study 100 desirable houses, we find that they all agree in one thing. They are planned to meet the needs of people with definite habits and purposes. So with poultry houses, the breed, conditions of feeding, climate, size of flock and purse, and other matters which concern the owner alone must be considered. Therefore, without trying to lay down any definite rules for poultry house building we give suggestions from those who have apparently solved the problem for their own conditions.

THE ESSENTIAL PRINCIPLES.—On the White Leghorn farm of White & Rice the following rules of house building are followed. This farm is 30 miles north of New York:

FIG. 19. WHITE & RICE'S HEN HOUSE.

"The three essentials in building a poultry house are comfort, convenience and cost, in their order. Comfort should be first, for the reason if the hens are not comfortable no amount of work and feed can make them lay in the Fall and Winter when the high prices of eggs make poultry keeping so profitable. Then comes convenience. Have things just as handy as you possibly can, for you will find when you keep a thousand and more hens that having houses handy to feed, water and clean will save many days' work in the course of a year. One hour a day means over one month in a year. Last of all comes the bugbear of so many, cost. Cost does not spell comfort or even convenience. There are many expensive poultry houses that are both uncomfortable and unhandy. A hen needs five square feet of floor space, and to keep her comfortable in cold weather we must build the house low so she won't have to warm up an unnecessary air space, but don't get it so low that you break your own head when caring for the hens. Very good dimensions for a single house are 12 x 15 feet, seven feet high in front and four in the rear.

"The floor should be raised six inches, with stones and a good cement floor put on that, making it proof against dampness and rats, two of the

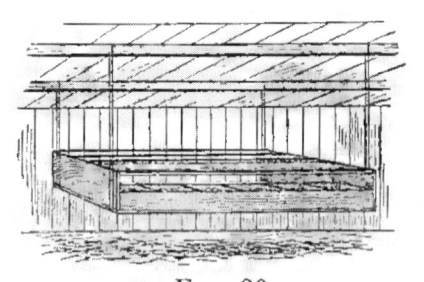

FIG. 20.
SWINGING ROOST AND NEST.

trials poultrymen are heir to. The sills and roof timbers should be 3 x 4-inch hemlock or spruce, and 2 x 3-inch stuff is heavy enough for all else. The siding and roof boards may be of any cheap lumber that is dry and free from loose knots. Cover the roof with three-ply tarred paper and a coat of roofing cement or paint. A modification of the colony house plan is the best (see Fig. 19). Building six houses together makes it more convenient to care for the hens, is warmer and costs less than single houses, while the flock is none too large to run together in the Summer. Strong unbleached muslin makes good partitions in such a house. It is also used a great deal for windows, being warmer than glass in Winter and cooler in Summer. The only thing against it is, it does not let in quite as much light on a dark, cloudy day as the glass will, but where they have very cold Winters it is the best thing to use.

"Have the interior of your houses as simple as possible for the sake of cleanliness. The simplest way is to make your nests under the roosts and suspend the whole device from the roof. Then there is nothing to bother cleaning the floor, and no cracks between roosts and side walls to harbor mites and trouble. For a house this size you would want a platform six feet long and three feet wide with three perches on, and a row of nests underneath (see Fig. 20). A shell or grit box, made like Fig. 21, is fastened to the wall so it is easily removable. The dust box, and water basin, complete the furnishing of the house. The scratching-shed house is particularly adapted to breeding stock, and is a little more expensive than the plans given here, but where you want the best results from your breeders it is worth the extra cost. In Fig. 19 you notice the windows are low and should be made of muslin tacked on stiff frames, the whole hinged, making a door when you wish, and always should be open when the weather permits. A six-section house would be be 90 feet long, accommodating over 200 hens, and should not cost over $150 complete if built on this plan. It will be so comfortable and convenient that with good feed and care you cannot fail to make poultry keeping profitable."

COLD-COUNTRY HOUSE.—Fig. 22 shows a section of the long poultry house at the Maine Experiment Station. This is located in a very cold country, and great pains are taken to make the

FIG. 21.
SHELL AND GRIT BOX.

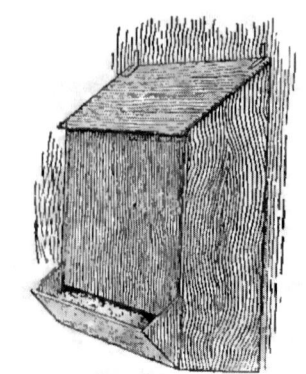

hens comfortable. This house is 14 feet wide and 150 feet long. The back is 5½ feet high and the front six feet eight inches. The ridge is nine feet from the floor. Fig. 23 shows the interior fixtures of one room, it being 20 feet wide. In this space—20 x 14 feet—50 hens are kept. The house is boarded, papered and shingled on roof and walls. The rear wall behind the roosts and four feet of the roof above are ceiled on the inside of the studding and plates, and the space between packed hard with dry sawdust. As will be seen from the picture, each room of this house has two 12-light windows screwed on to the front. The space between these windows, eight feet by three, is covered with wire netting. The lower part being boarded prevents the wind from blowing directly upon the hens. During stormy days and cold nights a curtain consisting of a light frame covered with 10-ounce duck swings down in front of the wire and covers it. The picture shows how this curtain frame swings from the top. The roost platform extends the whole length of the room. It is three feet six inches wide and three feet from the floor. The roosts are 2 x 3-inch stuff placed on edge and are two inches above the platform. They are 16 inches apart; the backs are 11 inches from the wall. Two curtains similar to the one in front are noticed hung over the roost platform. They are 10 feet long and 30 inches wide, hinged at the top and arranged with pulleys, so as to be pulled up or let down easily. Six trap nests, as are shown on page 15, are arranged in the corner as shown. The door leading to the next room is 2½ feet wide. This door is a light frame covered with 10-ounce duck, such as is used in making the curtains. It is made with double-acting hinges, so as to swing both ways—a great advantage in passing through such a house. Strips of old rubber belting are nailed to the studs, which the doors rub against so they will not swing too easily with the wind. The wire front of this house admits the air, but the hens do not feel the direct force of the wind. During rough Winter storms or on very cold nights the front curtain is lowered and fastened with a button, so that it comes in front of the wire screen, thus shutting out the wind and

FIG. 22.
COLD COUNTRY HOUSE.

FIG. 23.
INTERIOR OF ABOVE HOUSE.

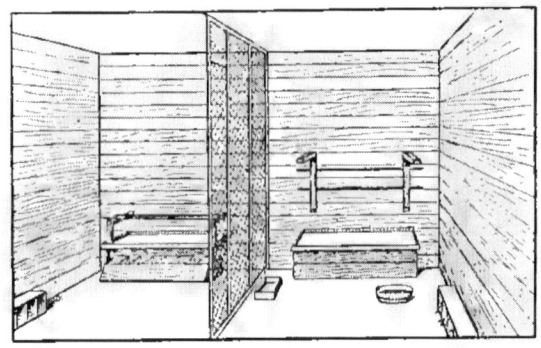

taking the place of windows.

The object of the curtains in front of the roosts is to make a warm room for the hens on very cold nights. On such nights, after the hens have gone to roost, the curtains are let down and buttoned, so that the hens are shut in a small room. The heat of their bodies keeps this room warm, and, strange to say, the air behind the curtains does not become foul. It is said that when these "sleeping closets" are used not a sick hen or even a case of bad cold could be found. After passing the night in this warm place the hens seem to enjoy coming down to the floor to scratch for their food in the litter. We would not recommend this "roosting closet" except for use on very cold nights. The plan of an open front with a curtain has much in its favor.

FIG. 24. VAN DRESSER'S PARTITIONED HOUSE.

HOUSE INTERIORS.—The interior fixtures for henhouses vary almost as much as do those for human families. Fig. 24 shows an interior of one of Henry Van Dresser's houses. A wire netting partition divides a large room in two. The arrangement of roosts and nest boxes is easily seen. Fig. 25 shows a little house used by Mr. Cosgrove, who lives in a cold part of New England. He describes it as follows:

"This is the most economical house to build that I know of. The house is 10 x 10 on the ground. A perpendicular front would (with the same roof) be only 7 x 10, so I gain 30 feet of floor surface at a cost of only 46 feet of boards. The house is made of seven-eighths-inch matched pine, roof and back covered with red Neponset roofing paper. There are no sills or plates; the boards are nailed to a 2 x 3 x 10 scantling six inches from bottom edge, and three inches below top edge, so that the ends of the 2 x 3 pieces that the roof is nailed to rest on the 2 x 3 that the sides are nailed to. Each part, top, back, front and sides are made separately, and are hooked together across the corners. The house can be unhooked, laid flat on the ground and loaded on a wagon in five minutes, and put together again as quickly. Two large windows which slide sideways allow nearly half of the front to be open

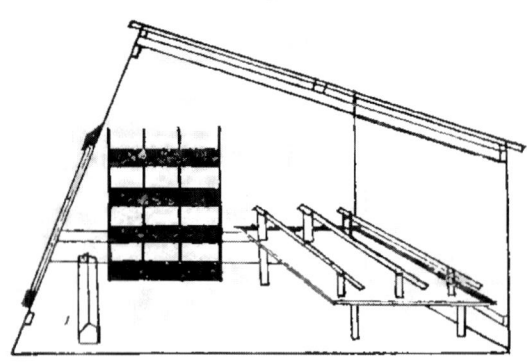

FIG. 25. COSGROVE'S MOVABLE HOUSE.

in hot days, as well as the large door in east end (which is left off to show interior) and which opens into an open front scratching shed size of the house. The low windows let the Winter sun shine on the earth floor, drying and warming it, so the fowls make a dust bath of the entire floor. Roost platform, with removable roosts, nest boxes and feed trough, are shown; on the east end next the door is a box with three partitions, one each for shells, grit and charcoal."

FIG. 26. SCRATCHING SHED ARRANGEMENT.

Fig. 26 shows a plan for connecting the house with a scratching shed. Fig. 27 shows how a boy with a small backyard kept a few hens in a piano box, while Fig. 29 shows a henhouse on wheels, often used in England for pasturing the hens on a grain stubble. This house or wagon is hauled about the field after harvest, and the hens pick up the grain that was lost by the reapers.

WARMING THE HENHOUSE.—Some experiments have been made in providing artificial heat. In Maine a house 150 feet long was well built, yet cold in the worst of Winter. A hot-water heater was placed in a pit at one end, and from it a line of two-inch pipes was carried the entire length of the building and returned under the roosts. This gave sufficient heat, kept the hens in good health, and the egg yield was maintained. Stoves have been used in some houses, but not with the best of success. A device for using a lamp in a small house is shown in Fig. 28. On a large scale, and in very cold weather, the hot-water pipe might pay, but the danger is in using the heat in milder weather—when the hens would be better off without it. Some poultry keepers follow the plan that has proved so successful with cattle; building a tight, warm building, providing for a good ventilation, and leaving the question of warmth to the animal heat of the hens. H. E. Cook has described what he calls a "hen sanitarium." This was a room 10 x 24 feet. In this room 125 hens were kept, and though outside the mercury fell to far below zero, the temperature inside ranged from 37 degrees to 42 degrees. Mr. Cook says:

"This house is thoroughly insulated upon all sides but one, which is protected by another building, by a stuffed wall of straw and straw above, and a cement floor, thus shutting off every chance for air to enter around the wall or for cold air contact or moisture from the soil below. I have repeatedly said that it does not seem possible to secure large egg production in the Winter in our northern sections, where it storms often three days in a week and

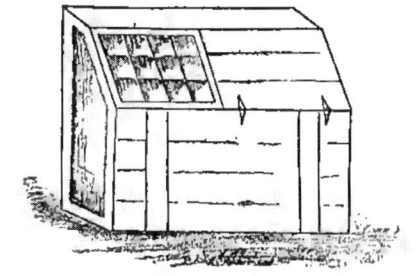

FIG. 27. PIANO-BOX HOUSE.

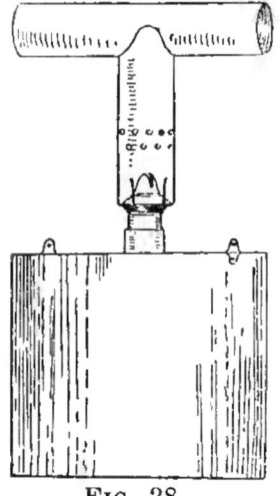

FIG. 28.
A LAMP HEATER.

is cloudy rest of the time, and this exceptional year these things things happen every day in the week. But this warm henhouse is giving 40 to 53 eggs a day for the past six weeks from 125 hens, 75 pullets, and 50 old hens, and 40 degrees below absolutely had no effect otherwise than to increase the production two eggs per day. This room is ceiled upon the inside with unmatched boards, the side walls filled with straw, about 10 inches space. In the loft straw is put in loosely, and the space between the boards caused by shrinkage is left open into the loose straw above The door into the room does not shut air tight, and therefore serves as an intake for fresh air; then very slowly passing into the straw above. In this way it would seem that a much slower circulation takes place than would if there was an opening cut directly into the loft and the circulation left free, as it would through even an ordinary out-take flue. I do not feel like speaking with much authority upon the hen business, but it is rather a lingering belief that henhouses as a rule are troubled with too much change of air rather than a lack of it, and furthermore that the apparent need of ventilation when one goes into a house comes largely from filth, and a lack of sanitation due to droppings long preserved. I am not inclined to belittle the necessity of pure air, but to magnify the value of cleanliness, and so secure pure air with less frequent change. There is ground for debate whether open dead air spaces are preferable to stuffed walls. My preference is for the stuffed space, provided it is wide enough, for this reason: Each straw is hollow and cannot be absolutely (if dry) packed so closely to another that there will not be air between them, and hence with this means of insulation there will be provided a multitude of dead-air spaces, at moderate cost, while to secure even two spaces with lumber at $20 per 1,000 means rapidly increasing cost and there certainly should not be less than two. Furthermore, no lumber can be so sound and thoroughly seasoned that there will not, even if painted, be some shrinkage after a few years' use, and when these. previously considered dead-air spaces have openings they are no longer dead-air spaces, because air circulates in them and heat is quickly carried away. A mistake, however, is often made when stuffing is to be practiced in forming the space too narrow. It should ordinarily be not less than 10 inches, more or less, perhaps, accord-

FIG. 29.
HOUSE ON WHEELS.

ing to wind pressure against its sides. When plain dead-air spaces are used, then one-half inch will suffice as well as more. I am of the opinion that the ceiling will be better if the lumber is not matched, thereby leaving small cracks to be covered with two or three feet of dry, loose straw."

It will be noticed that Mr. Cook allows less than two square feet of floor space to each hen, but the greatest care is taken to have this floor clean. The litter is changed frequently, and the floor is swept often, which is possible, since it is made of concrete. The manure is cleaned out before it becomes offensive. It would not be possible to keep the hens in health in such crowded quarters if the house were not kept so clean. We have many other reports of hens crowded into a small space and yet laying remarkably well. In every such case the houses are well ventilated and kept thoroughly clean. It seems to be settled that we may safely use the animal heat of hens or cows to keep up the temperature of their rooms if we can provide for a supply of pure air and dispose of the foul air without creating too much of a draft.

FIG. 30.
HAYWARD'S 14-HEN HOUSE.

THE DUST BOX.—This ought to stand in the sunshine out of all drafts; under the front window is a good place. Road dust is excellent. It is well to secure a quantity of it during a dry spell in Summer. We have found dry sifted coal ashes good. A large shallow box is best. Do not fill it too full so the hens will kick the dust over the floor. In some cases a small quantity of lime is added to the dust, but we do not like it, as it takes the gloss from the feathers. Do not let the dust remain too long. It must not become damp or caked. In freezing weather the dust box should be emptied frequently, so as to keep the dust dry.

THE FLOOR.—Good arguments are advanced for cement, board or earth floors, just as different housekeepers prefer carpets, matting or rugs with hard wood. The wood floors are warm and easily cleaned. Cement makes a solid floor, and if properly built keeps out rats and vermin better than the others.

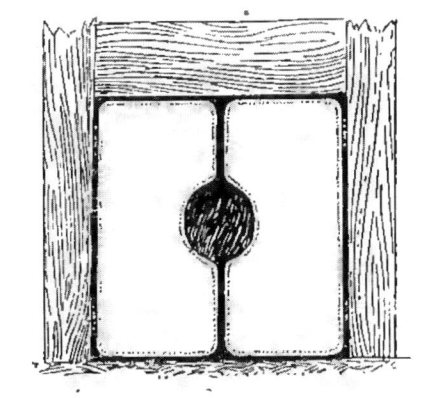

FIG. 31.
SWINGING HEN DOOR.

It is easy to clean, the chief objection being that it is cold. With plenty of litter this objection counts for less. Earth floors can be dug over from time to time, and make a good natural place for the hens to dig and dust. After some years they become foul, unless dug out and changed yearly, and are more likely to carry disease germs than floors that can be easily swept clean. Unless well drained they are wet in rainy weather. A combination liked by many is a cement floor covered with several inches of sand or dry dirt. Whatever floor is used a good covering of clean dry litter must be kept on it and frequently changed. Cut straw makes good litter; so do forest leaves or shredded cornstalks. Oat straw in the sheaf is used by some poultry keepers.

ROOSTS.—Notice how a hen holds on to the perch and balances herself upon it. A square strip with the edges rounded off gives her a better grip than a round pole—a two or three-inch strip, according to the size of the bird, will answer. Do not put them too high. The hens are often hurt by flying up to them. The arrangement shown on page 50, used in White and Rice's house, is excellent. There should be a dropping board one foot under the roosts to catch the droppings. The roosts should not be fastened, but put in notches so that they can be quickly taken out for cleaning. In some cases duck or other thick cloth is tacked to the under side of the roosts. This will be kept smeared with kerosene, and thus prevent the mites from gathering there. The dropping board must of course be cleaned off frequently. Its great value is that the hens can run under it, and thus have greater floor space.

BARNS FOR HENHOUSES.—Sometimes a farmer wishes to change from dairying to poultry-keeping. Men often buy farms with large buildings used formerly for sheep or cattle. How can such buildings be made over to suit poultry? While it is better to build houses exactly suited to hens this is not always possible, and the larger buildings can be used. A Maine man fitted up an old building, and this is what he says about it:

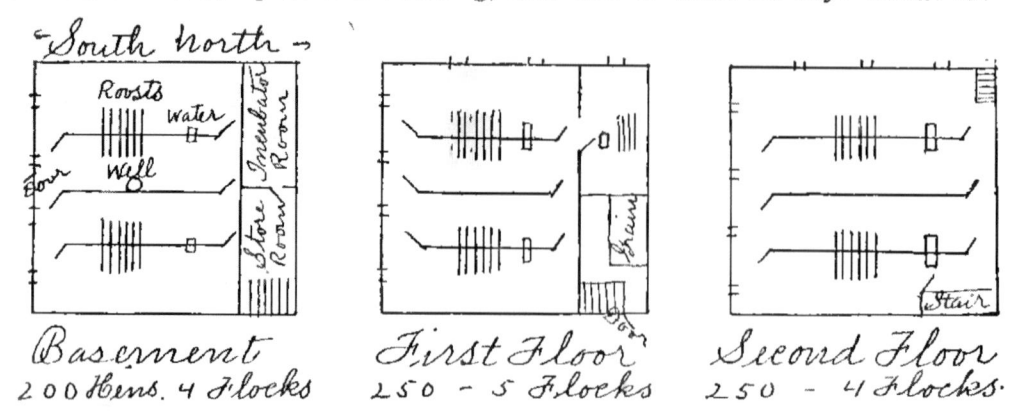

Basement — 200 Hens. 4 Flocks   *First Floor* — 250 - 5 Flocks   *Second Floor* — 250 - 4 Flocks.

"I have used and am still using a barn 36 x 40 feet as a three-story henhouse. The lower story is a basement open to the south; second floor is on the level with all the land except south of barn; third is up one flight from entrance. In Summer I let each floor run as one flock, having a large field and orchard, and only have division fences running about 300 feet, and I find that a hen very rarely gets around the end. The upper flock have a run which starts about 10 feet from end of barn, and runs through the middle pen to the ground. I use poultry wire for partitions and doors. I have no walks, and have doors rigged with pulleys and weights so that they keep shut. Troughs are made of 10-inch boards for mash, and I feed dry grain on floor in litter. Water dishes are elevated on a wide board about 12 inches from ground, which keeps water clean. For roosts I use 2 x 3-inch pine planed and simply laid on stringers two feet from the ground, which makes them easy to clean, and roosts are placed so that two flocks roost close together. Sometime I want to use the space over the big beams as a pigeon roost to raise squabs. I am only using two floors this Winter, as I have but 400 hens, but I would not exchange my barn for any henhouse, as the work is all in a bunch.

CONFINE HENS.—Fig. 30 shows one of the 600 houses on the poultry farm of C. E. L. Hayward, Hancock, N. H. The houses are eight feet square and of the same height, having a double floor with a square base 15 inches high of two-inch plank, to which the roof boards are nailed. The roof and back are shingled. The front is boarded down from top and up from bottom about 15 inches. The door and spaces each side are covered with wire netting one inch mesh. Thus the south end is nearly open to the weather the year around. The houses are in rows two rods apart, four rods between the rows, all facing the south. Each house has 14 hens. No chickens are raised. In October and November every hen is sold and a new stock of pullets, raised by contract in Vermont and Canada, put in.

CHAPTER X.

Feeding the Hen.

A BALANCED RATION.—Nothing connected with poultry keeping requires more skill and judgment than giving the hen what she needs to make feathers, flesh and eggs. A farmer who just throws corn out to the hens now and then will say feeding is easy, and there is no skill about it. He is wrong, for the hen furnishes the skill and judgment. She eats the corn, and then goes out and hunts for insects, seeds, grass—anything that she can find. If we could gather everything she selects in this way and analyze it we would find that it makes a "balanced ration," much the same as the mixture of grain and meat which the skilled feeder gives his hens in the Winter. To prove this statement we have only to remember that in Summer, when the corn-fed hen has a chance to balance her ration she lays eggs. In Winter, when still fed corn but denied the chance to hunt for insects and meat she quits and lays on fat. I know a farmer who for years fed corn in Winter and had few eggs. He bought a bone cutter and fed cut bone, and had a good supply. Why was this? The cut bone enabled the hen to balance her own ration as she did when she hunted insects to go with the corn. The idea of a balanced ration was suggested first by an effort to imitate the hen's natural food, when she is shut in a yard or house. It is based on the fact that certain parts of the hen's body cannot be produced unless certain distinct elements are supplied in the food. For example the shell of the egg is composed largely of lime. It will not be made of any other substance, and unless lime is supplied in some way there can be no shell. The feathers, the white of the egg, the muscles and lean meat of the hen contain an element known as nitrogen, and the food must contain a fair supply of this muscle-making material. The chemists call this part of the food protein, but we will call it here muscle-maker. The fat of the body is made from starch, sugar, and similar materials in the food. The muscle cannot be made from these fatty foods. If we feed too many of them the hen will stop making lean meat or laying eggs and simply lay on fat. We will call this part of the food "fat formers." There is also a quantity of oil or pure fat in most foods. It is more digestible than the fat formers and we call it "pure fat." Left to herself, with plenty to choose from, a healthy hen will make a nice selection of these three elements in her food, taking enough "muscle makers" to keep up her bone and muscle and provide for the egg, and enough of the others to suit her purpose. Human mothers need the doctor or some other wise man to come and tell them that their children

Feeding the Hen.

should eat oatmeal or other whole grain to provide the material for teeth and bones. The hen knows by instinct what she needs, and in order to cater to that instinct, when we cannot let the hen choose entirely, we get the chemist to pick our grains and other foods apart so that we can tell how to mix them and give the hen a good Winter imitation of her Summer diet of worms, seeds and grass. For the hen must have mineral matter to build her bones and shell her eggs. This "mineral matter" is the part of the hen or her food which cannot be consumed by fire, but which remains as ash. We must also remember that the hen cannot utilize all the food she eats. More than half of its fertilizing value passes away in the form of manure. We must give her food enough to provide for all.

AMOUNTS IN TEN POUNDS OF EACH.

	Muscle-makers.		Fat-formers.		Pure fat.		Ash or Min. Mat.	
	P. C.	Ozs.	P. C.	Ozs.	P. C.	Ozs.	P. C.	Ozs.
Wheat bran	12.	19.2	39.	62.4	2.7	4.4	6.4	10.2
Wheat	10.	16.	69.	110.4	1.7	2.7	1.8	2.8
Corn	8.	12.8	67.	107.2	4.3	6.8	1.4	2.2
Oats	9.	14.4	47.	59.2	4.2	6.7	2.9	4.6
Rye	10.	16.	67.	107.2	1.1	1.7	1.9	3.
Middlings	12.5	20.	53.	84.8	3.4	5.4	3.3	5.28
Gluten meal	25.	40.	43.	68.8	11.	17.6	12.	19.2
Meat meal	40.	64.	7.5	12.	10.	16.	38.	6.
Beef scraps	50.	80.	5.	8.	21.	33.6	15.	24.
Clover hay	7.	11.2	36.	57.6	1.7	2.7	62.	9.9
Buckwheat	7.7	12.3	49.	78.4	1.8	2.8	2.	3.2
Skimmed milk	3.	4.8	5.	8.	0.3	0.48	0.7	1.1
Eggs	12.	19.2			10.	16.	14.5	23.2
Cut bone	21.	33.6			32.	51.	22.	3.5
Barley	9.	14.4	65.	104.	1.6	2.5	2.7	4.3
Millet	9.	14.4	45.	72.	3.2	5.1	2.6	4.1
Sorghum	7.	11.2	52.	83.2	3.1	4.9	1.5	2.4
Sunflower seed	12.	19.2	21.	33.6	29.	46.4	2.6	4.1
Linseed meal	28.	44.8	40.	64.	2.8	4.4	6.	9.6
Peas	17.	27.2	52.	83.2	0.7	1.1	2.6	4.1

WHAT IT MEANS.—It does not take us long to see why, when the farmer added cut bone to the corn his hens laid more eggs. A dozen eggs will weigh not far from 25 ounces, requiring three ounces of muscle makers, and nearly four of mineral matter. Ten pounds of corn do not provide half enough mineral matter for the dozen eggs, even if every bit of the corn could be used and none passed as manure. The muscle makers are also low in the corn, and when the hen provides for the growth of body and feathers, animal heat and the fat necessary for comfort there is not much left in the corn to furnish the material for eggs. We see what happens when cut bone is added. This is rich in muscle makers and mineral matter, and the hen was ready to provide for the needs of her system and also lay eggs.

It does not follow from this that cut bone and corn is the best ration for hens just because it gives her mineral matter and muscle makers. You can put water in a steam boiler and burn coal under it and make steam, but a hen is not fed that way. Like most humans she prefers one kind of food to another, and will do best on food that she likes. You must study her likes and dislikes and cater to them.

FIG. 32.
HINGED FEED BOX.

Why, then, talk about "balanced rations," and what is the need of studying these figures? You cannot always afford to feed the hen just what she likes best. You must often substitute one food for another. How can you know that you are feeding the hen more or less than she needs unless you can know just what the foods contain? If you could figure out what the hen eats when at liberty and what the most successful hen keepers feed their birds when housed, you will find that there is a definite proportion of muscle makers to the other elements. If we call the fat worth 2½ times as much as the fat formers and add the two together we shall find that there is about ¼ as much of the muscle makers in the ration. That is, when the laying hen is left free to select the food that will best keep up her body heat and vigor, and enable her to lay eggs she will select about one part of the muscle makers to four parts of fat formers and pure fat, with, of course, plenty of lime and other mineral matter. If you were fattening poultry you would of course mix up a ration that would contain more of the fat formers.

This in brief is the theory of a "balanced ration." No one expects a farmer to feed his hens on exact scientific principles, but a little study of these figures will often enable us to mix our feeds so as to save grain and keep the hens supplied with what they need. Successful poultrymen have different methods of feeding, but if we know what they feed we shall find that the mixture comes close to our "balanced ration," which is a good thing to take for the standard.

TWO WAYS OF FEEDING.—To illustrate two different methods of feeding hens we give a report from the Maine Experiment Station of feeding in cold weather when the hens are housed:

Years ago the "morning mash," which was regarded as necessary to "warm up the cold hen," so she could lay that day, was given up and it was fed at night. The birds are fed throughout the year daily as follows: Each pen of twenty-two receives one pint of wheat in the deep litter early in the morning. At 9.30 A. M. one-half pint of oats is fed to them in the same way. At 1 P. M. one-half pint of cracked corn is given in the litter as before. At 3 P. M. in the Winter and 4 P. M. in the Summer they are given all the mash they will eat up clean in half an hour. The mash is made of the following mixture of meals: 200 pounds wheat bran; 100 pounds cornmeal; 100 pounds wheat middlings; 100 pounds linseed meal; 100 pounds gluten meal; 100 pounds beef scrap. The mash contains one-fourth its bulk of clover leaves and heads, obtained from the feeding floor in the cattle barn. The clover is covered with hot water and allowed to stand for three or four hours. The mash is made quite dry, and rubbed down with the shovel in mixing, so that the pieces of clover are separated and covered with meal. Cracked bone, oyster shells, clean grit, and water are before them all the time. Two large mangels are fed to the birds in each pen daily in Winter. They are stuck on to large nails, which are partly driven into the wall, a foot and a half above the floor. Very few soft-shelled eggs are laid, and, so far as known, not an egg has been eaten by the hens during the last five years.

We are testing another method of feeding with several pens of hens this year. It consists of the morning, 9.30 A. M., and 1 P. M. feedings of dry food in the litter as usual, but instead of the mash at 3 P. M. all the dry cracked corn they will eat is given in troughs. Beef scrap is kept before the birds at all times, in elevated troughs where they cannot waste it. They are supplied with grit, oyster shell, bone, and mangels. Dry clover leaves and chaff are given them on the floor each day. One pen of 30 hens were fed through last Winter in this way with good results.

If you figure this out by the table, multiplying amount of "pure fat" by 2½ and adding to the "fat formers," you will see that the mash contains the following:

	Muscle Maker.	Fat Former.	Pure Fat.
200 Wheat bran	24	78	5.2
100 Corn meal	8	67	4.2
100 Linseed	28	40	2.8
100 Gluten	25	43	11.
100 Beef scraps	50	5	2.1
	135	233	25.3

This is a proportion of about one to three and the corn, oats and wheat will just about give a proportion of all the food ot one to four. We feel quite sure that the hens which are fed on dry food eat enough of the beef scrap to give about the same proportion. We do not give this ration as a model one, but as an illustration of how hens can be fed. It will pay to go over any ration in this way and see just what the hens are receiving. We should have a few definite principles in mind, and then try to satisfy our hens. There may be cases where skim-milk is cheap and plenty. If we used it in place of water we should need less linseed or meat, as we can learn from our table. In many cases corn is by far the cheapest food. We can safely use large quantities of it if we use some form of meat with it to provide the needed muscle makers. Taking care not to have the proportion of fat formers in our ration too large, we should feed to please the hens, making them work for most of their food, and when once getting them satisfied making changes very slowly.

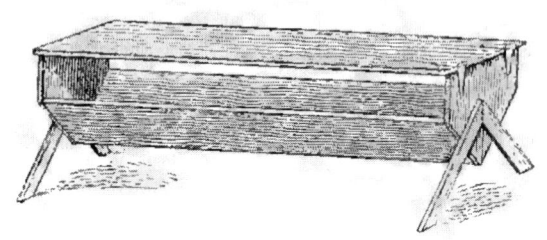

FIG. 33. HANDY FEED BOX.

Another method of feeding hens in Winter quarters is given here. This is useful on a dairy farm where skim-milk is handy:

"In the morning they are fed about 10 quarts of dry feed in the litter in scratching sheds, the litter pushed up into a heap, and the grain scattered through it so they must scratch; the grain is usually half cracked corn and half wheat, sometimes oats in place of wheat, sometimes buckwheat, but always half cracked corn. As I have two hundred hens, this is a light feed, about one pint to ten hens. I want them hungry enough to work. Early in the forenoon eight quarts of skim-milk are placed on the back of the kitchen stove, where it will heat without burning, and at noon this is poured into a large iron kettle, together with two quarts of animal meal, a tablespoonful of salt and three times a week a teaspoonful of red pepper; then stirred into it all it will wet thoroughly of bran and cornmeal, two parts bran to one of meal. It makes eighteen quarts of feed, all the hens will eat up clean. About every other day three or four quarts of boiled potatoes are cut up and mixed in the milk. Just before sundown they are fed the same dry feed as in the morning, only more in quantity. I aim to feed at this time all they will eat. For green food cabbages are fed three or four times a week. The above shows what is fed, and how much, but as a matter of fact, each coop is fed differently; and I do not know of anything more difficult for the novice to learn than how properly to feed fowls. Last night I sent my boy, 14 years old, to feed the hens; this morning, an hour after the hens were off the roosts, in three of the coops there was still a lot of feed in the troughs. That means no scratching, no work, sitting around half the day in a bunch; and if that sort of thing was kept up it would soon mean few if any eggs. My fowls have had no green cut bone, no cut clover, no bought grit; doubtless all these things would be good for them, and might increase the egg yield, but my experience shows that very good results can be obtained without them. I keep ground oyster shells and fine gravel gathered from the wash by the roadside and sifted, also broken charcoal, in each coop all the time."

FEEDING HINTS.—The mash is useful, as it gives a good chance to feed fine meat or to give ginger or pepper and salt when needed. No single grain has just the right feeding "balance," wheat and oats coming nearest to it. We can make the mash into any proportion we like. By using a good proportion of corn meal we can get the hens to eat many cheap forms of food which they would not care for alone. For example, wheat bran and gluten, two useful feeds will be eaten when mixed in a mash but not well when fed alone. The common mistake is to feed a thin slop in place of a dry, crumbly mash. The hens rightly object to the former. We have tried the experiment of feeding a well-balanced mash alone. The hens did not respond as they did when the same mixture of grains and meat was baked into a hard cake and crumbled for them. The hen does not chew her food like other animals. It is ground up in her gizzard by sharp stones or grit which she swallows. The hen does not seem to thrive for any considerable time when all work of grinding her food is taken away. Part of the ration should be in the form of dry grain. When hens are laying fast the mash is useful because the food it contains is quickly available. The hen can utilize it at once. She may not get it fast enough if compelled to grind all her own grain.

Experiments have been tried in letting the hens balance their own ration by keeping a variety of food constantly before them. In our own experiments this proved a failure. Some of the hens grew dumpy and lifeless, while others remained active and fresh. They laid well for a time, but the general observation is that after a time the self-balancing system fails. With us the chief trouble was that the hens missed the incentive of hunger. With food always before them they saw little need of scratching or working and became lazy, as most men would under similar circumstances.

We conclude that most hens are more likely to eat too much of the fat forming foods if given a chance to do so. They are not so likely to eat too much of the muscle makers, hence the plan suggested of keeping beef scrap before them and regulating the feeding of corn or other grain will work better than the plan of keeping all before them. It is wise to remove what the hens leave of the mash after ten or fifteen minutes of eating. It is likely to sour in hot weather, and it is a good plan to make the hens understand that eating is a matter of business.

GRAIN FOOD.—Corn is preferred by most hens. Throw down a mixture of all grains and they usually pick out the corn first. When properly "balanced" with meat or other forms of muscle makers corn is the best grain we have for poultry. If fed in the form of whole or cracked grain entirely some of the hens will eat little besides corn, and will put on fat when they ought to lay. That is one reason why a mash or a baked cake composed of a mixture of grain and meat is very useful for part of the ration. As we might naturally expect, corn is the best single grain for sitting hens where the object is to keep up the high animal heat, and for feeding birds that are intended for fattening. Corn gives a high color to the yolks of the eggs and to the meat. Wheat comes much nearer to being a "balanced ration" than corn, and where it can be bought to advantage is very useful. We can use our table of figures to learn whether it will pay best to buy wheat or with the same money buy corn and some form of meat. Wheat alone gives an egg with a pale yellow yolk. We find that wheat bran, which is the outer shell of the wheat kernel, has much the same effect. Oats are excellent in limited quantities, but are seldom bought to be fed whole, and on most farms are considered better for the horses. We have heard complaints when dry oats are fed in large quantities to hens. We would rather crush them to mix in the mash or boil them if fed whole. Some experienced poultrymen say that oats give "spirit" to a hen as they do to a horse, and for that reason are very useful—better fed whole than crushed. Oatmeal is a favorite food for little chicks, the same as for young colts or calves. Buckwheat is largely fed in some sections where the crop is grown. Hens probably give a better return for whole buckwheat than any other stock. Outside of buckwheat sections it would hardly pay to buy this grain. It is a stimulating food, as many people realize who eat too many buckwheat cakes. On the average farm corn is the chief food for hens, and the usual problem is to find some cheap supply of muscle makers in order to "balance" the corn. The advice to throw the whole or cracked grain into the litter in Winter so that the hens must scratch in order to find it is sound, and is the general practice. If this is done, however, the litter must be clean and dry. If we let the straw, leaves, hulls or whatever is on the floor get damp and filthy we should not throw the grain there. Such filth will give just the conditions needed to spread disease. We should never throw the grain into the mud or into filth. If we feed in the litter we must have clean floors with the litter frequently changed.

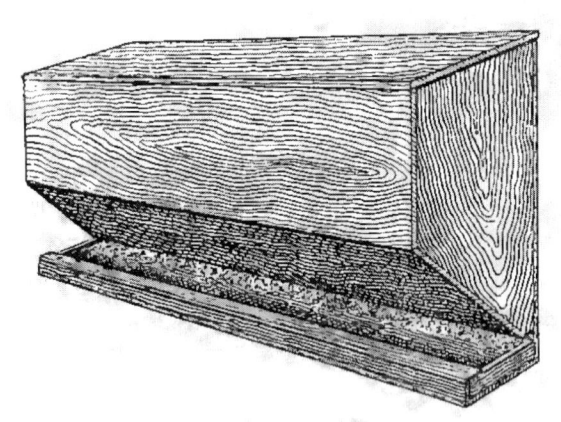

FIG. 34. SELF-FEEDING GRIT BOX.

MUSCLE-MAKING FOODS.—Meat in some form may be considered a necessity in the laying hen's ration. Left to herself the hen gets her supply in the form of insects. "Animal Meal" and similar powders are cooked meat and bone thoroughly dried and ground fine. They give a high per cent of muscle makers and may be thoroughly mixed in the mash. Cut bone is a very useful food which is not usually mixed with the mash but fed by itself. It consists of green or fresh bone, sliced or shaved into thin pieces by a bone cutter, which is turned by a crank and cuts or gouges off the end of the bone. Where a good supply of fresh bone can be obtained this cut bone is very useful. It cannot be kept sweet like the dry animal meal. We have seen cases where part of the carcass of a dead animal was hung up in the henhouse for the fowls to pick at. In cold weather it will keep reasonably sweet, and it is surprising to see how the hens will pick the bones clean. In some cases bones are roasted and smashed as well as can be with a sledge. Any form of meat is likely to loosen the bowels of the hen when first fed. Especially with cut bone or when feeding a carcass, the hens should be watched carefully and not fed too much. Linseed meal and skim-milk are often used as substitutes for meat but do not really take its place. Linseed is a laxative food and should not be fed heavily. Skim-milk is one of the most valuable of foods.

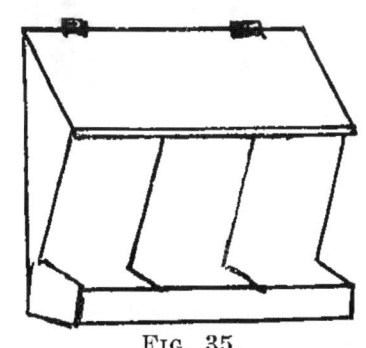

FIG. 35. ANOTHER SELF FEEDER

Some farmers go so far as to say that young pigs and chicks cannot be properly raised without a supply of milk, but facts do not warrant the statement. The milk is very useful for mixing the mash or for feeding alone. We should always provide fresh water even when feeding milk. The feeding value of skim-milk has been demonstrated in boarding-houses and public institutions. Whenever the boarders are provided with all the milk they desire, the meat bill always falls off. Still, no one but an infant can depend on milk alone to supply all needed muscle makers.

VARIOUS FOODS.—While we do not regard green food as a necessity in hen feeding there is no doubt that the hen feels better when provided with grass or a substitute for it. Cabbage is the usual salad fed in Winter. It may be hung up by a string so that the hens must jump up to get it. The fact that they *do* jump for it proves that they crave something of the sort. Beets or mangels are often fed, either chopped in two so that the hens can pick at them on the floor or hung on a nail driven into the wall. Clover hay is relished by the hen, and not only gives her a bulky food, but supplies muscle makers and mineral matter. The chaff and heads which fall on the barn floor when the hay is thrown down may be mixed in the mash. Some feeders chop the clover hay into short lengths, steam it thoroughly by pouring boiling water upon it, and then covering it up. It is fed hot in the middle of the afternoon in Winter, and we have seen hens devouring it as cattle would. Clover and Alfalfa are sometimes ground into a fine meal, which is excellent for mixing in the mash. Fish may be fed in moderate quantities to hens before it begins to decay. It can be cooked and thrown down for the hens to pick over. We must remember that the food has a decided effect upon the flavor of the egg, and that decayed or foul-smelling stuff will surely taint the egg. Sunflower seeds can be fed in small quantities. They, with buckwheat, are useful just before and during the hen's moult. It is thought by some that sunflower seed will actually hasten the moult and induce the hen to shed her feathers early. While cotton-seed meal is fed in some parts of the South, we do not advise its use in the average flock. Linseed or some form of meat is much safer. Boiled beans or cow peas are relished by hens. We prefer to feed them mixed with boiled potatoes or corn meal.

GENERAL ADVICE.—A vigorous hen in full laying will eat about five ounces of well-balanced food each day. What is called a "maintenance ration" means the amount of food actually required to keep up the body of the hen without laying or gaining in flesh. When a mature hen stops laying and becomes idle 2½ or three ounces of food will be ample for her needs. When hens run in an orchard or in a grass park in the Summer it is a wise plan to feed the whole grain in the grass, sowing it broadcast, as one would for seeding. The hens hunt and scratch for it, and if not overfed will get it all. The exercise is just what they need, and they find many bugs and eat much grass while hunting for the grain. A mixture of equal parts of corn, oats and wheat is good for this broadcasting. Hens like a variety, and some will pick out corn one day, oats another and wheat at another time. Where hens can run at large they pick up 40 per cent or more of their food. The skilled feeder comes to know when they have had enough. Hens of the different breeds vary in their food habits. The lighter breeds, like Leghorns, seem to be more intelligent than the heavier fowls, and are not so likely to over-feed. The Leghorns will stand a heavy feeding of corn better than Plymouth Rocks or Brahmas. The latter should have a fair supply of meat and seem to require green food even more than the lighter fowls. Some authorities have claimed that it is not necessary to keep oyster shells or other supplies of lime before the hens, because the food contains enough of that substance. The hens do not agree with these authorities, for they empty the shell boxes and would not do so if the lime were not needed. We should keep a full supply of lime before them. Ground bone is excellent for this purpose, but in the Eastern States oyster shells are usually cheaper. It is the practice of some farmers to haul a load or two of shells from neighboring fish markets every year. These are scattered on the ground in front of the barn, and the wagon wheels and horses' hoofs grind them up gradually. The hens help themselves as they feel inclined, and if the shells do not wear down as fast as needed a few minutes' work with an old hammer will hurry them along.

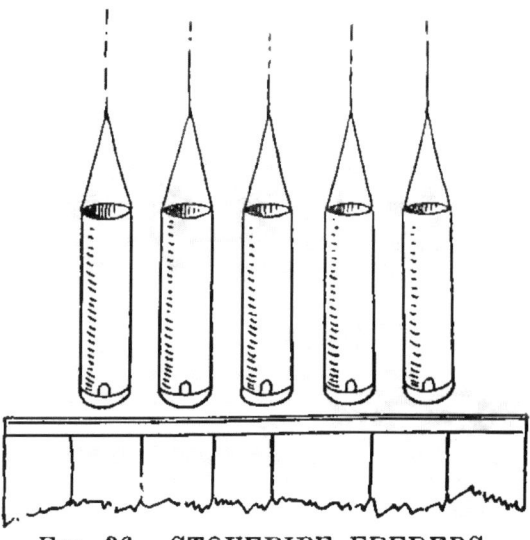

On sandy land hens will generally find all the "grit" they need. The object in supplying this "grit" is to furnish the sharp little stones which, in the hen's gizzard, grind up the hard food. There is no grit in the little chick as it leaves the incubator, and it must be supplied in the brooder. That is why many poultry keepers keep the bottoms of the brooders covered with clean, sharp sand. Some of the "chick foods" consist of mixed grains and a quantity of crushed stones, the latter furnishing the chicks with the needed "grit"; of course the hens must be supplied with fresh water, for they drink frequently, and we must remember that over 60 per cent of the egg is water. Avoid a drinking dish that the hens can walk into. A covered feeding dish for the mash is best, one that only permits the hen to put in her head. Salt in small quantities helps the hen, but it is a poison when used to excess. It is more necessary when hens are yarded than when they run at large. The proper feeding of a hen can only come through long and patient experience. It "looks easy" but proves a hard job.

FIG. 36. STOVEPIPE FEEDERS.

The best feed troughs have a cover which protects the food and prevents the hens from stepping into it. Two good forms are shown at Figs. 32-33. These are hinged at the side or end, so that the cover is easily raised for cleaning. A convenient self-feeding box for shells or grit is shown at Fig. 34. Another simple style of self-feeder appears at Fig. 36. This is made from pieces of stovepipe. They are closed at one end, with small holes cut at the side near the bottom. They are hung from the roof by means of wires, so that the bottom hangs near the roost platform. They can be used for feeding charcoal, shells or grit. A drinking fountain made by inverting a tin can over a smaller dish is shown at Fig. 37. For those who do not care to bother with homemade devices, excellent drinking fountains may be had from all dealers in poultry supplies, and they are so cheap and durable that no one need be without adequate means for supplying hens and chicks with pure water.

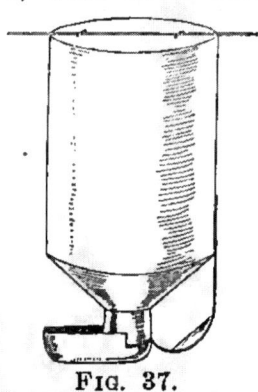

FIG. 37. DRINKING FOUNTAIN.

CHAPTER XI.

The Colony Plan.

By this is meant the plan of letting the hens run at large in a field. They are housed in small buildings scattered about the field—40 or 50 to the house. Mr. O. W. Mapes keeps about 1,500 hens on the colony plan, and the following story of one day's work will give a good idea of the way such a farm is conducted. Mr. Mapes selects the best hens for breeders, and they are kept by themselves in small houses. Under this system, while the hens mingle during the day, they usually go back to their own houses at night. The colony system is best adapted to the production of Summer eggs. Mr. Mapes does not claim a heavy yield in Winter, yet with his systetm of handling his hens averages a profit of over $1 each per year. This is the way the work is done.

"My son and partner proposes to take full charge of the poultry and pigs, while I care for the cows and horses. This will give us a chance to form some opinion of how much poultry it would require to furnish a full day's work for a man, under better and more ideal conditions. He was up about five o'clock, and had things well under way when I reached the barn. While breakfast was being prepared he proceeded first to mix his morning batch of feed for the hens. There are 1,482 of them, and he dumps four baskets of balanced ration into the box on the old buckboard. This weighs 35 pounds to the basket, making 140 pounds in all; 100 quarts of skim-milk are then poured on it, and the whole well mixed with a shovel. This takes about 15 minutes. I have found the following mixture to give very satisfactory results both where fowls have free range and when confined in yards with nothing else whatever in the way of food, not even green food of any kind. Oyster shells, grit and water were supplied, of course, but I hardly class those as food: Wheat bran, five pounds; wheat middlings, five pounds; cracked corn, 10 pounds; cornmeal, 10 pounds; animal meal, two pounds. To this should be added enough skim-milk to wet into a mash. It makes a very good mixture without milk, using water instead, but milk is an improvement. For small chicks the cracked corn should not be very coarse. It is as well to use coarse ground cornmeal in place of cracked corn for the small chicks. For larger chicks and for hens I prefer the cracked corn in order to give the gizzard a chance to perform its normal functions. He passes the end of the long brooder house on his way to breakfast, giving a pull on the end of a long wire projecting out through the siding. This takes about two seconds, and raises the small drop doors in each of the 10 brooder apartments, admitting about 1,000 chicks to the outdoor runs for exercise, fresh air, etc.

FEEDING THE CHICKS.—"The first job after breakfast is to feed the chicks in the brooder house. A barrel of balanced ration and a can of skim-milk stand convenient in the long hall as he enters. This hall runs the whole length (rear) of the 60-foot building, and is four feet wide. The first two pens contain about 100 chicks each that are four weeks old. For these he dips about 1½ pound of feed in his basin, and pours on enough skim-milk to wet it. After giving it a few stirs with his big iron spoon he is ready for business, but not more ready than the chicks on the other side of the wire partition. To those who are not accustomed to it, the feeding of 1,000 chicks is an interesting sight. To us who are used to it it is only work. It requires a little skill to open the gate and step into a pen of 100 hungry chicks, without stepping on them, or allowing any of them to jump out into the hall. See him dash a morsel of feed through the wire gate, to the farthest corner of the pen. The wild scramble which follows furnishes his opportunity to step inside and allow the spring to close the gate behind him. A hundred pairs of wings are instantly spread, and as many of his white pets land on his basin as can get a foothold. Brushing them gently aside, he places half of his feed in the trough, giving the remainder to the chicks in the next pen. Pens 3 and 4 contain about the same number of chicks that are three weeks old. For these he mixes a little less of the feed, still less for pens 5 and 6, which are two weeks old, and about 12 ounces for pens 7 and 8, which are only a week old. Pens 9 and 10 are reserved for next hatch, now coming out of their shells. They will get water to drink, and bread crumbs moistened with milk to eat for first four or five days. After that they get same as the rest, and nothing else whatever except grit and water. This ends the morning duty for the chicks.

INCUBATOR WORK.—"The incubators come next. These are in another building, partly underground, also used as a shop. The first thing he does on entering is to light a lamp and take the reading of the thermometers. No. 1 read 103 degrees. These eggs have been set a week, and this heat would have been all right a few days ago during the hot wave, but it has now turned decidedly colder, and he gives the set screw a slight turn to the left. No. 2 is hatching to-day, and is not to be opened. The chicks are crowding against the glass door so thick that it is almost impossible to see the thermometer. Passing to No. 3 he reads 104 degrees. The animal heat in these eggs has raised the temperature since yesterday, but in view of the change in weather conditions, this is all right. The trays of eggs are next removed to the long work bench, the eggs turned and allowed to air while the lamps are trimmed and filled, when they are returned to the incubator and the doors closed.

THE HENS.—"It is now 6.30 A. M., and he is ready to feed the hens. By the time he has done a few odd chores about the barn, harnessed his horse to the buckboard, and got under way, it is seven o'clock. His tools are a small fire shovel for dipping the wet mash, a large iron spoon for scraping any dirt from the troughs and a couple of feed pails. A medium-sized shovelful represents 12 ounces of dry feed, and his aim is to allow a shovelful of mash to each eight hens. Glancing at the figures on the inside of the door of pen No. 1 tells him that this flock contains 49 hens (last count) and he gives them six shovelfuls of mash, and opens the small drop door which allows them free range and a drink of water at the brook or pond. There are 35 flocks, and this is repeated until all are served. He finds a few troughs that are damp, showing that yesterday's supper had not been all eaten until morning. These have their allowance slightly reduced. By eight o'clock he is back to the barn, and has a couple of pails of feed left in his box. We have settled down to two feeds a day of this mash for the hens, and nothing else except what little grass, grit, water, etc., they find in the fields. Price of wheat and corn has got so high that we find the balanced ration at $30 per ton is less expensive, and I expect less sickness and better health than where grain is kept constantly before them. Jesse only found two dead chicks under the brooders this morning, and no dead hens. This is less than our usual mortality. Crushed oyster shells are always kept scattered about in abundance.

PLAN OF BUILDINGS.—"The houses I use for laying stock are only 10x12 feet on the ground, with shed roof. The front is eight feet high, and faces south. The north side is five feet four inches high. On the south side is a door for general use, a small drop door 6x8 inches for hens to pass in and out, and one good-sized window. The large door is near the east end, the small door near the middle, and the window near the west end. This permits the afternoon sun the greatest sweep of floor space in Winter. The table for droppings is 2½ feet above the floor, and extends along the whole north side of the room. Under the table, on this north side, is cut a small door 2½ feet high and one foot wide. Aside from this, the house is as near airtight and windproof as matched boards and building paper will make it. The small door under the roosting table on the north side is kept tightly closed in Winter, and in Summer it is protected with wire cloth and kept open. This permits a free current of air to circulate through the house and out at the open window on the opposite side, without striking the hens on the perches above the table. I formerly kept 40 hens in each house, but recently have increased to 50 each. The 1,500 hens probably roam over nearly half of our farm of 70 acres, as their roaming ground covers quite a distance from the buildings in all directions.

BROODER LAMPS.—"Next on the programme come the trimming and filling of the brooder lamps. These rest on the floor, and are put under the brooders from the hall, through large openings in the partition, leaving them exposed to full view from the hall, and giving them plenty of pure, cool air. A long shelf at convenient height contains an oil can, matches, lamp-rag, etc. The lamps are lifted to the shelf, the screw cap removed and filled. A puff of the burning lamp tells him when it is full. The oil can is always left open so that no gas can gather in it to cause an explosion. Now the lamp is extinguished, the hinged burner turned back without removing the tin chimney, and a sharp knife drawn across the top of wick tube, removing soot, charred wick, etc. As soon as the burner is wiped clean, care being taken to remove all particles of dirt from the perforated brass which admits fresh air to the flame, the match is applied. The burner is still hot, and the piece of emery paper above the shelf is so located that the same stroke which ignites the match, brings it across the top of the wick, and lights it, without waiting to see whether the wood of the match is going to ignite. Five quarts of oil and 15 minutes' time are required for the 10 lamps. They will need no more attention for 24 hours. The brooders in Nos. 9 and 10 must be got ready for the chicks now hatching. They are scraped as clean as possible, smeared with kerosene as a preventive of lice, and the floor under the hover covered with sand. They will be nice and warm by the time the chicks are ready for removal to-morrow. The drinking fountains are next filled with fresh water, and the regular morning work is accomplished by 8.30 A. M.

PACKING EGGS.—"The work of cleaning, stamping and packing the eggs for the market usually falls to some of the women folks, but Jesse relieves them of it to-day. There are 845 eggs in the baskets gathered yesterday. These are first placed in a large tin pan, and sufficient lukewarm water poured over them to cover them. With a washrag spread over the palm of the left hand he takes them out of the warm water one by one with the right hand, gives one end of the egg a turn against the cloth-covered palm of the other hand, reverses and gives the other end of the egg a turn, laying them in regular rows on a thick soft cloth covering the long table on which he works in the wash room. An occasional egg that is badly stained is laid one side, to be recleaned later on with vinegar or sapolio. The heat retained from the lukewarm water in the pan causes them to dry quickly as they lie on the soft cloth, retaining the peculiar glow of the new-laid egg. Before he packs them in crates, each egg is touched with a small rubber stamp, made on a very soft air cushion, placing the name and address of the producer on its shell. Every egg we ship to market is expected to carry a little bit of character with it, and send back in return a little bit of extra cash. It will take him about two hours to clean and pack the 845 eggs, and while he is doing it I drive to town with our regular shipment of eggs, and bring back our regular supply of skim-milk. He would have had ample time for this also. The advent of wife and baby has not spoiled his zest for the boyish sport of fishing. Long before my return from town he is at the pond, with rod and gun, looking for a mess of fish, and a large hen hawk he has had his eye on for several days. The chicks two weeks old and less got a light lunch of feed before he started out, from the same barrel as for breakfast. The older chicks were getting hungry, too, but must wait for their regular three meals a day.

AFTERNOON WORK.—"After dinner the same routine of feeding the chicks is gone through as in the morning. He now has time on his hands again until three o'clock, and improves the opportunity to clean up his buggy and harness. At 3 P. M. the buckboard is again loaded with mash for the hens, using about 20 pounds less than for the morning feed, since a little was left in the box. The hens are at liberty this time, and come to meet him in large numbers, the wagon often being covered with the greedy white beauties. This is the weak spot in feeding a number of flocks that have free range. A little practice, however, enables one to apportion the feed quite uniformly.

EVENING FEED.—"The pigs get their supper (same as breakfast) as soon as the hens are all fed, and at 4.30 Jesse starts out with five big baskets to gather up the eggs. It takes him a few minutes more than an hour to gather them and carry them up to the house, and he has 804 as the result of the day's work. By 5.45 the chickens are again fed, and the eggs in the incubator turned. This finishes the day's work, all except pulling the wire in the brooder house and closing the entrances to the henhouses. He has used 260 pounds of feed, costing at $30 per ton, $3.90, and 4½ cans of skim-milk, costing 10 cents per can, for the hens. This is a total of $4.35. The market quotation for eggs to-day is 17½ cents. We get five cents per dozen above market quotations, for our guaranteed eggs at present 22½ cents. The 804 eggs, which is rather under the daily average for the past week, are thus worth $15.07, leaving a margin of profit of over $10 aside from my prospective profits in the growth of the pigs and broilers. This is not a big story, but it has the merit of being literally true. When our henhouses were first built, we used to close the entrances at night by pressing an electric button. The expense of keeping the battery charged, and the trouble of keeping the line in perfect order has caused it to fall into innocuous desuetude. We are now arranging to drop and raise the doors by pulling a wire, after the plan in use in our brooder houses."

CHAPTER XII.

A Market Gardener's Hens.

We, that is my wife and I, own a small farm of 30 acres, which we are devoting to a variety of interests; chief of these are the growing of small fruits, market garden and truck crops; but we also keep two cows, about 20 hogs, a dozen hives of bees and a flock of from 125 to 130 hens. We have kept accurate records, and find that in four years during the six months that require more or less housing the flock has averaged 37 eggs to each 100 hens per day. The flock comprised quite a number of older hens a part of the time. A difference is plainly seen in the last year of the table below, when the entire flock consisted of pullets. The number of dozens laid each month is as follows:

	1899. 1900.	1900. 1901.	1901. 1902.	1902. 1903.
November	29	53	47	59
December	64	97	74	90
January	145	107	115	153
February	143	94	100	167
March	162	138	163	201
April	162	138	150	189

There has been something of a variety of breeds in this flock. Good grade mongrels with a large dash of Leghorn blood, purebred Barred Plymouth Rocks, Black Minorcas and White Wyandottes all figured largely in the flock at some time during the period, and they showed very little difference in their laying qualities. What slight difference I could detect was to the credit of the Wyandottes, and the entire flock is now composed of that breed. As the hens have occupied the same quarters, and the treatment has been practically the same during the whole period, I will describe both in detail. Small fruits and truck crops are grown in considerable quantities; these are largely sold at retail, and between managing the work in the fields and marketing the crops my time is pressingly occupied during the Summer; but as we do not board the help my wife, who is a true lover of hens and chickens, rears the young stock and takes general oversight of the poultry department. Under her care the pullets are always in prime condition in the Fall. Only Summer crops are grown, and the men are hired only for the busy season. So after the season is closed by frost in the Fall there is no produce to market but eggs and butter, and these are sold at wholesale and sent by a neighboring butcher. Our market, Harrisburg, is eight miles away. Then, being relieved from the press of Summer work, I give my first attention to the care of the hens and other live stock. To show how well such work may be made to pay even in a small way, I will state that the gross receipts at present for the butter and eggs from two cows and 130 hens are at the rate of about $60 per month. The five or six hours each day that are not required for this work I usually devote to pruning and general preparations for the next season's work.

WINTER MANAGEMENT.—Having on hand the proper number of hens or pullets—the latter preferred—well-bred, well-reared and vigorous as possible with the first approach of uncomfortably cool weather in Fall they are confined to their houses in the early morning and on stormy days. As the season advances they are shut in entirely, except that when the weather is fine and there is no snow they are occasionally allowed to run in the yard for 10 or 15 minutes, and then returned. During mid-winter they have been constantly confined for two months at a time with no bad results. The entire flock is housed in two separate apartments which are by no means ideal. The larger of these is a room 12x28 feet, arranged in the northwestern end of the basement of a bank barn. Necessarily the windows are in the northwest and southwest sides; hence, they are not well adapted for the admission of either sunshine or ventilation. These defects are reduced by a door which opens to the southeast under the "overshot" of the barn. This door is fitted with a screen, hence can be left open when necessary. The rear wall of this room of course is of stone, the other three are of matched boards. The floor consists of packed clay, except a section 12x12 feet in the rear, which is of boards; this is occupied by the roost. As may be supposed from its location, this room is just barely dry enough not to give trouble. The smaller is a house of the common shed-roof construction, measuring 7x30 feet. This is built of rough boards and battened. It has a good exposure, but is too high and narrow, which makes it colder than it would otherwise be. The floor is of clay throughout. The roost in this house occupies a space of 7x10 feet. In each house the perches are low, 18 inches, are built in one piece trestle fashion and rest on the floor, so they are easily kept free from lice and moved for cleaning the house. Besides the roosts the furnishings in each house consist of a row of a dozen nest boxes, a self-feeding shell-box, a galvanized iron trough for water, a box for the dust bath and several wooden troughs for feeding mash. There is nothing about the buildings that may not be arranged or built on almost any farm at moderate cost. The space not occupied by the roosts is covered with a litter of forest leaves, in which all the grain is fed. I have never found anything near so well adapted to the purpose as leaves.

GENERAL CARE.—Once a week the floors are thoroughly cleaned, the manure is scraped up, the soiled litter removed, the whole floor swept and then fresh leaves put in. This is very important, and must not be postponed, as nothing will cause hens to lose their tone and vigor more quickly than eating from foul litter. Of course ventilation is freely given by opening windows or screened doors so as not to cause a draft. In severe weather all is kept close, ventilating thoroughly two or three times a day when the hens are busy. Clean water is given every morning and warm water added when cold enough to freeze. The dust bath is renewed once in two weeks. No roosters are kept in the flock. The food consists of corn, oats, wheat, cornchop and bran, beef scrap, cabbage, hay and milk. The quantity the hens will eat varies with the number of eggs produced; but last Winter, when the flock was at its best, and the quantity of food had been the same for more than a month, I took a note of the exact quantity, and comparing this with the amount fed this season since they are in full laying condition I find it is practically the same. The quantity for 100 hens per day is about as follows: Corn, 3½ quarts; oats, six quarts; wheat, five quarts; cornchop and bran, mixed equal parts by weight for the mash, six quarts; beef scrap, one pint every second day; cabbage, three or four small to medium heads. About a peck of hay shatterings, mostly clover, such as collects where hay is thrown down, is given every few days.

FEEDING SYSTEM.—Not less important than the variety and quantity of food is its proper distribution throughout the day. In this it is well to remember the conditions in the Spring that usually induce the laziest hen to lay. The warm weather, new grass and insects coax her out, and she eats all day long, but only a little at a time, she becomes interested and busy. This is the vital point. No moping hen ever laid many eggs. With these facts in view the hens are fed little and often, six times in a day, as follows: Early in the morning they are given 1½ quart of oats. They wake up and take some exercise scratching for this, and then at eight o'clock they get their mash. At 10 o'clock 1½ quart of oats are again given and the same at 2 P. M. The noon feed consists of two quarts of wheat, and the evening feed, which is intended to be all they will eat, is 3½ quarts of corn, three quarts of wheat and 1½ quart oats. The cabbage is invariably fed in the evening after the grain. Milk and beef scrap are mixed in the mash. I have found mangels a fair substitute for cabbage. Caution should be exercised not to overfeed either of these or any other "greens," as it is sure to cause a derangement of appetite. It will be noticed that oats are fed in small quantities and often. I consider them a very important part of the ration on account of their bulk, but experience has made me cautious of feeding any large quantity at a time. Now, to those not accustomed to giving any but the most ordinary care to their hens, the foregoing may seem like all too much "fuss and feathers" to obtain eggs even in Winter; but the hen trust has its price and it is doubtful if eggs can be had in quantity for much less. After all if the work is done methodically it is not such an endless round as may at first appear. Thus, in beginning the morning chores, I first give the hens their bit of oats, a "scratch" we call it, after doing the other work the mash is given. The noon feed comes in with the rest of the stock feeding. The evening chores are begun by giving the hens their grain; then after gathering the eggs the cabbage is distributed. This leaves no extra running after the chickens, but to give them their "scratch" at 10 and two o'clock. This requires but a few minutes when I am about the barn, and when in the field pruning or absent from home my wife says it gives her exercise as well as the hens. Some one will be sure to ask what is to be done if the hens lack appetite. I must say I have had little trouble in this line. It is natural for hens to eat heartily if conditions are right. If they are fed lightly and often during the day, with a full feed at night, a proper ration of proper bulk; if protected from drafts and floors are kept clean; if, when making a change of food, care is taken to feed sparingly at first there should be little trouble. I have never had anything so serious but what was easily corrected by feeding scantily for a day or two. Perhaps the old saying: "Eternal vigilance is the price of success" does not apply better anywhere than to managing hens in Winter, but I think where the vigilance is exercised the success is sure.

HOMEMADE GRAIN SCREEN.—Examine a sample of cracked corn and you will be surprised to see how much fine meal it contains. When this feed is thrown on the ground most of the meal is wasted, as the chicks cannot pick it up easily. Mr. J. E. Stevenson saves this waste by using the device shown herewith. A hopper is arranged at the top of the stairs. Screens one foot wide and three feet long are made out of three sizes of wire netting. These screens run under the stairs and the hopper feeds into the coarser one. These screens sift the corn into three sizes and save a good share of the meal.

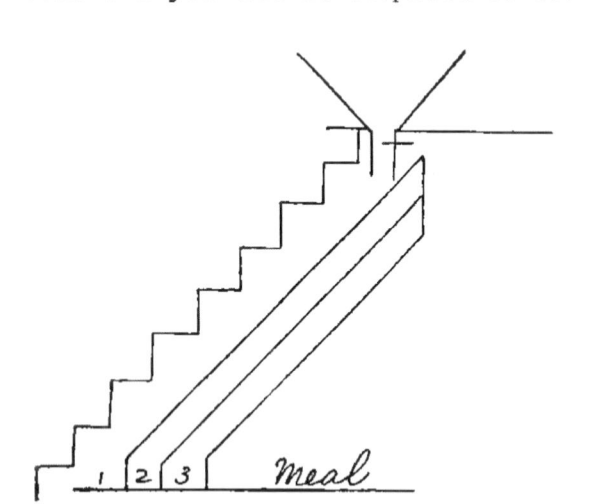

CHAPTER XIII.

The Boy's Hens.

We moved to town one Winter and were able to hire a small henhouse. We had sold the best pullets on the farm, and had left only a mixed lot of old hens and young roosters. We took about 20 of these birds to town, killing and eating them from time to time. Early in February there were only three hens left, and the little boy begged for them, so that he might try "the chicken business." His best argument was that the table scraps would nearly feed the hens, thus turning what we would not eat into what we would be glad to have. I thought he would soon tire of it, but to my surprise he became interested, and gave his hens good care. By mixing a small amount of wheat bran with the scraps he kept the hens laying and in good condition. When I saw that he had become interested enough to work for the hens I knew that he had caught the chicken fever. An industrious hen may lead a lazy boy into habits of hustle. I told the boy that if he could make his three hens lay 13 eggs in a week, I would start him with a larger flock. The next week they laid 15 eggs. Of course the boy, like most beginners with poultry, felt sure that if he could make three hens lay well, there is no good reason why he could not do as well with 30, 300 or 3,000. It takes a large unpaid grain bill to cure one of that idea.

BUYING HENS.—We went to New York for new hens. Those left on the farm were poor specimens, and the boy wanted to try different breeds. I have bought live poultry in New York many times. One year I bought 150 hens and pullets, and imported roup, lice and various other troubles. Eggs from those New York hens cost me eight cents apiece through January and February, but they laid fairly well in the Summer, and just about paid for their feed and original cost. I conclude that hens usually sent to the live market are just about such culls as we had at the farm. It stands to reason that no one will knowingly sell a good laying hen for meat any more than they would sell a good Jersey cow for beef. We found one place where a number of good hens had been sold to close out an estate, and the dealer, who knew a good hen, had sorted out the best to sell as layers. Crowded into his coops and fed nothing but corn, they were laying eggs enough to pay for their food twice over. After much debate the boy bought three Brown Leghorns, three White Wyandottes, one White Leghorn and one Light Brahma. As it turned out he would have done better if he had bought all Brown Leghorns, but he wanted to test the different breeds. You may read about such things, but **it is better to learn from your own experience!**

STARTING THE HENS.—These birds came out by express, and the boy was all ready for them. He had bought a package of "chicken powder" which looked like a mixture of fine tobacco and sulphur. He took one hen at a time, held her up gently by the legs and dusted the powder into her feathers, taking care to work plenty of it under the wings and around and under the tail feathers, and along the neck and shoulders, as these are the hardest places for the hen to reach. The boy learned from the poultry dealer not to run or shout at a hen if she gets away, or to pull and shake her if she flutters in your hand. You must be as gentle as possible with your hens if you expect them to lay. The laying hen is active, lively and nervous, but she does not want you to string up her nerves. The boy expected that when his 11 hens were put together in the house they would act like sisters, and have only one ambition—that of laying eggs! Instead of that the three original hens singled out the Light Brahma and attacked her vigorously. Hens often show these strange dislikes, and when taken to a new place they always "dry up" for a time and will not lay until they feel at home. The Brown Leghorns were first to call their new place home and begin to lay. The White Wyandottes followed, but the Light Brahma was very slow..

FEEDING A SMALL FLOCK.—The table scraps and wastes and parings from vegetables and fruits gave these hens more than half the food they required. In order to provide the remainder the boy mixed the following: Two parts by weight of wheat bran, one part cornmeal, one part of wheat middlings and one-half part animal meal. This was fed in the form of a dry crumbly mash in the morning, with a good handful of clover heads and leaves mixed with it. The hot water used for rinsing off the breakfast plates was good to dampen this grain. Wheat bran is one of the best grains for hens, but they do not like it when fed alone. Of all grains corn in some form is best relished by poultry, and cornmeal or cracked corn should go in the mash. There are only two good reasons why a mash should be fed—it gives a good chance to provide warm food and enables us to feed meat in the right proportion. I am quite sure that the mixture of grain and meat baked into a cake and crumbled up for feeding would pay better than a soft mash. The boy fed whole corn at night, and made the common mistake of most beginners of overfeeding his hens. He kept too much food before them. Some of it soured. The hens lost their ambition to work and hunt for food. The Brown Leghorns held their ambition longest, because it was part of their breeding, but what hens or men ever do their best when they know the good things of life are being wasted on them? It took the boy some time to learn what every feeder must know, that the hens must be made to scratch for most of their food. Maybe the boy learned something about his own habits of industry by watching these hens. Some things at least he did well. He kept plenty of clean water and oyster shells before the hens at all times, and he kept the house clean. The hens responded—at least some of them did—and owing to the low cost of the table scraps gave us eggs that cost less than half a cent apiece while they were worth four cents in the local market.

A LARGER FLOCK.—Of course the boy, like all poultrymen, wanted a larger flock. Somehow we all come to think that if we could only have more land, or more cows, or more hens, we can make growth on our ability as we do on our stock. When we came back to the farm the boy found nine more hens, and a White Wyandotte rooster. The hens were a mixed lot, but the rooster was a good one. They had all had a hard Winter, sleeping in the barn or in an old henhouse without much care. The old farm chicken-yard was to be used as a garden, so the boy cut poles in the woods and helped to build a new yard at the back of an abandoned ice house, which was a henhouse years before. He dug holes for his posts, and then a six-foot chicken fence was tacked around with a baseboard nailed at the bottom. We have tried piling stones around the base, but this does not answer. The boy made clean nests of straw, dusting them well with his chicken powder. The roosts were not nailed down, but put in sockets, so that they can be lifted out and cleaned easily. Every morning he took a pickax and spade and dug up the ground in the yard, thus providing worms for the hens. There were many leaves and parings in the table scraps, but the boy pulled grass and weeds and fed them freely, for hens like green food. The boy began to understand something about the different kinds of lice that make hens miserable. The little mites that pass the day on the under side of the roost are bad citizens—night robbers, for they crawl up at night and attack the hens. We can make life a burden to them by keeping the under side of the roost well smeared with grease. Every now and then the roosts must be taken out and washed with boiling water, and then painted with kerosene. The large gray lice that stay on the hens are easier to fight if we give the hens a fair chance to keep clean. A vigorous hen will dust in the dry soil or in a box of dry coal ashes and free herself of most of these lice. A good dusting with some "chicken powder" or fine tobacco will finish up. I know of people who read somewhere that kerosene is the thing to kill lice with, so they took some hens and rubbed kerosene over them! They could not have done a worse thing, for it took hide and feathers off the hens. A mixture of lard and sulphur rubbed under the wings and at the base of the neck will help, but do not put pure kerosene on the hen. The boy found that there is little use fighting the lice on the hens if the building is neglected. Most old farm buildings are alive with vermin, which breed in filth, so that they must be kept clean. The manure ought to be scraped out twice a week at least. In spite of the "chicken powder" the nests will soon be alive. The hay or straw should be taken out and burned, and the boxes painted with kerosene before new nests are made. The whole inside of the house should be scrubbed out with boiling water, and whitewashed or sprayed with kerosene. The boy found to his cost that you cannot afford to neglect these things in an old house. He also found that some old building fitted up in this way cannot be made equal to a house built especially for hens.

KEEPING UP THE FLOCK.—The boy started with the notion that "a hen is a hen," without much regard to her breeding or age. He had heard some one say that "a hen is a machine," and he knew that we can use the mowing machine and hayrake for many years. He was grieved to find that some of his hens were sad loafers. Three of those he bought in New York ate their fill of grain, and then instead of heading for the nests stood about dumpy and lazy. What was the matter with them? They and four of the farm hens proved to be at least four years old, and probably six. They were like our old mowing machine—worn out. One day the men dug through the yard to get at a cracked water pipe under the barn. They threw out thousands of worms. These old veterans ate so many that the next morning five of them were found dead, with their crops stuck full. The boy buried his beloved hens around peach trees, and with many tears learned that age in a hen is not entitled to respect. When Grandmother failed to step about as spry as her daughters we expected it, and were all glad to give her the most comfortable chair and the best light. The hen is sure to fail with age just as Grandmother did, but we do not keep her for the good she has done. So the boy began to understand that he must plan for new pullets each year and dispose of the old stock. He now saw that the hens he bought in New York were probably birds that had done their best, laying for some one else, and were then sold for meat. We are also likely to have accidents in the flock. One good hen tried to fly up to a high roost, but failed, and fell and broke an egg inside of her. She had to be killed. This taught the boy to have his roosts down low, and made it clearer still that we must have young pullets each year.

PICKING OUT LAYERS.—Having seen the need of young hens the boy began to see that one young hen may be better than another. He could see that the men and boys we hired to work on the farm did not do an equal amount of work. Some did more and better work than others, though all wanted the same wages when working by the day. Sometimes the man who did the poorest job of work would eat most, or break most tools. There seemed to be much the same difference in hens. The Light Brahma waited nearly a month before she laid an egg, though she ate her full share, and then laid a dozen in succession. One of the Brown Leghorns proved to be lazy. Of course the boy did not want any more drones. It may be fun to feed a lazy pet hen when some one else pays for the feed, but when it means a loss of your own money, you soon get tired of it. The boy began to see if he could pick out the layers. He found it was not hard to do so. You can catch most of them on the nest. They go around singing and scratching, and the egg-layers are usually the liveliest hens and the best eaters. It is not safe to go by any single one of these signs. Sometimes a hen goes on the nest with no intention of laying. The lazy Brown Leghorn made more noise after laying one egg than the other two did over three, and the Light Brahma and the lazy Wyandotte ate their fill and then moped on the roost. You cannot tell layers by any one test, but after a good study of the actions of the hen you can pick them out. The boy had specimens of four different breeds in his little flock, and he found that all these breeds contained workers as well as drones. Before long he learned that half the hens did more than three-fourths of the laying. It was good business to eat the eggs from the lazy hens and keep those from the workers for setting. The boy had noticed how many children there are who "look like father and act like mother." This is the principle of breeding which hen men ought to learn by heart. The boy will learn later that some of the old hens may be good breeders, though their granddaughters may outlay them.

BREEDING TO TYPE.—At first the boy though it wise to set eggs from all the best layers, no matter what color and shape they might be. Then he remembered that the poultryman wanted a dollar apiece for the Leghorns, while the spotted hens of all shapes and colors sold at a price per pound. Whenever people told him about a man who was doing well with poultry he was sure to find on that man's farm hens of one color and much the same shape. In years before, when we had all sorts of pullets, no one cared to buy them, but when we had bred pure Leghorns and Wyandottes a dozen people were after them. That showed him that if you expect to get the best price for your hens you must have them uniform, with the marks of some well-known breed. A spotted hen may be a fine layer, but you cannot make a buyer think so as you could if the hen were well marked, and had the true shape and appearance of one of the breeds that people know about. For instance, suppose you have Brown Leghorn hens and a White Wyandotte rooster, and you hatch the eggs from your best layers. The pullets may "act like mother" and lay well, but they will "look like father" and be spotted with all colors. No one would pay as much for such birds as they would if a Brown Leghorn rooster had been used. It is always an advantage to have birds that are salable as well as good layers. The boy began to see that if he was ever to have a flock of hens to be proud of he must make them as near alike as possible, and hatch the eggs from the best. He finally made up his mind that he liked the Brown Leghorns best. When asked his reason he said:

"They lay well. They do not eat as much as the others. They are tame and not so "scarey" as the Whites. They do not try so hard to get out of the yard, and they are pretty!"

As he grows older he will see a few more virtues and many more defects than he now sees in the Browns. For instance, the very fact that these little Brownies are so pretty with their varied plumage makes it all the more difficult to breed them true. This was his first idea of a "type" of hen that suited him, and I encouraged him in it, because it is the foundation of success to try to develop and maintain the things that we love and admire.

As the boy studied his hens he found that two of the Brown Leghorns laid well, while the other was something of a shirk. One of the hens laid a much larger egg than the other, and as the small size of the egg is one of the weaknesses of the Browns the boy decided to keep all of the large eggs he could for hatching, keeping close to the principle that he wants his coming pullets to "act like mother." He wants to save his money and buy a good Leghorn rooster.

Thus the boy begins to pick up the first principles of successful poultry keeping. He is working out on a small scale some of the problems of selection and feeding, the mastery of which have given men fame and fortune. These successful men grew into their success just as the boy is growing. At one time they knew less than he does. The reason they succeeded is that they kept on growing and learned to reason things out for themselves. One man may start with an old shed and a flock of mongrels; form his idea of type and select for it; study the wants of a hen and her comfort and grow into a comfortable business. People will pay for his care and thought when wrapped in feathers just as they pay for an author's thoughts when printed and bound into a book. Another man may start with the finest flock of purebred hens, go by printed rules alone, make no personal study of the hen, and fail. One man has hen in the heart—the other hen in the first layer of the head.

CHAPTER XIV.

Marketing Poultry Products.

The professional poultryman, who keeps in close touch with his market, knows its peculiar requirements and the problems that each season brings. The man with only a few hens as a side issue, raising say 50 or 100 chickens, is seldom so well informed on market matters, and may make mistakes that cut his profits in two. He may have sold through a careful dealer, who has told him how to dress and pack, or through a commission man of a type that takes whatever comes, and sells for what it will bring, without giving the shipper any tangible suggestions that might help make his offerings more salable.

The first requisite in shipping poultry to a large market is to have something worth selling, and the next is to know a commission man who is worthy of selling it. Such a man is found only through experience, either one's own or a neighbor's, and when found he is worth sticking to. He will appreciate this, and in 10 years more money will have been made than by scattering the shipments about.

In sections having a Hebrew population there is a steady demand for live poultry. which must be slaughtered under supervision of their official butchers.

FIG. 38. CRATE OF LIVE POULTRY.

The trade is heaviest at seasons commonly known as Jewish holidays, movable feasts. The exact dates for any year may be learned from dealers in live poultry. The principal feasts are the Hebrew New Years, Feast of Tabernacles, Feast of Laws, and Passover. In New York the receiving stations are centralized, and from these distribution is made to butchers. Fig. 38 shows a crate of live poultry, and Fig. 39 a lot of crates as piled on a wagon in West Washington market ready to be carted to the East Side Jewish sections where Kosher meat is sold. Fig. 40 shows a typical retail shop. The cuts of rooster and animal's head in the window indicate that officially prepared meats are on sale there. In the basement door the artist has inserted a scene familiar before the recent regulations forbidding the exposure of meats on the street. The market woman is dissecting a fowl for a fricassee while the customer waits. This work is now done under cover.

Broilers are received in market live and dressed, the latter dry-packed

FIG. 39. LOADING UP.

or iced. At Fig. 41 is a favorite crate for shipping live small chickens. Those shown weigh from 3½ to 4 pounds per pair. Though many lighter are sold, the best prices are paid for those about the weight mentioned. The crates are made of hard wood and are very durable. Some are 2½x3½ feet, and eight inches deep. Fig. 42 is a box of dressed broilers as put up by the meat-packing houses for shipment in refrigerator cars. The boxes contain two or three dozen according to size. Other poultry is also put in similar boxes. The farmer who ships in small quantities and does not have the advantage of refrigerator cars must ice his dressed chickens unless very near market or in cool weather. At bottom of page 85 is a barrel of iced poultry minus the burlap covering. In warm weather the icing must be thoroughly done and the ice in close contact with the birds. This makes them wet and messy, but they can be wiped off and dried so as to look very well. There are various expedients for doing away with this bad appearance, such as wrapping each bird in heavy paper, but this is only partly effective, and about the best way is to pack alternate layers of cracked ice and poultry, and a good sized chunk of ice on top.

As a rule the farmer is most interested in the Fall and Winter poultry market. He has something to sell for Thanksgiving, and clears out the rest of his surplus for Christmas and New Years. For Thanksgiving trade the weather is generally cool enough so that dry packing is safe. Boxes get rougher usage than barrels, being harder to handle, but a barrel is not so convenient to pack in. Unless sending a very small quantity it is best to sort the poultry, putting hen and tom turkeys in separate packages, and the culls by themselves; or better, keep the culls to get in condition for a later market. If boxes are used, they should not be too large. Less

FIG. 40. A "KOSHER" MEAT SHOP.

than a barrel in bulk is preferable. In very heavy packages there is some bruising from rough handling by freight or express men, who seem to think that a heavy box is an invitation to them to do their worst. Various rules for packing have

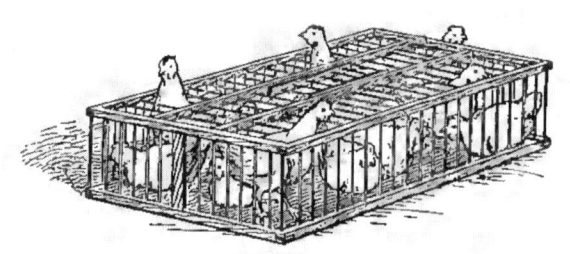

FIG. 41. A COOP OF BROILERS.

been given, such as putting them all one way, all breasts up, etc., but it is not always convenient to do this with long-geared turkeys, and about all that can be done is to fit them into boxes or barrels in whatever way they will fill up the space so as not to shake about. Some pack in layers with straw or heavy paper between, which may be some advantage, although straw, unless entirely free from chaff, sticks to the birds and is a nuisance. The safest way in packing is to follow the directions of the man who will handle the poultry, as market requirements differ, and he may have good reason for special preferences.

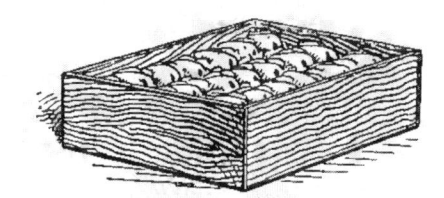

FIG. 42. DRESSED BROILERS.

In dealing with a large market it is necessary that the poultry arrive early. In smaller towns, where the shipper sells direct to the retailer, less margin is needed, but in New York most of it must go through the wholesaler's hands. Poultry for Thanksgiving should be on hand not later than Monday of that week, and the latter part of the previous week is better, as many retailers stock up then. If there is a scarcity, so that retailers cannot get supplies early, late arrivals may find a good demand, but the probabilities are that they will have to drag through the trade dullness always following a holiday.

New York, Philadelphia, Baltimore and Chicago demand undrawn poultry with head and feet on. The crop should be removed unless empty, but all poultry should be without food for several hours before killing. For Boston trade the general rule is to remove head, crop and entrails, making as small an incision as possible, and leaving in heart, gizzard and liver. Part of the neck should be cut off, the skin drawn over, tied and trimmed neatly.

FIG. 43. ICED POULTRY.

86   *The Business Hen.*

FIG. 44. METHOD OF KILLING POULTRY.

The Massachusetts law forbids the sale of undrawn poultry except where there is no food in the crop or entrails, an excellent law from a sanitary standpoint. Pittsburg demands drawn poultry with heads and feet off.

The best method of killing is sticking in the mouth with a sharp knife, while the bird hangs up by the feet. Here is the way it is done by one practical man. The picture shows the bird in the proper position. The wings may be locked together at the back by bringing one over the other and hooking the tip of the top wing under the other. The head is held in the left hand, the knife in the right. The knife should have a good sized handle with the blade keen and sharp pointed. Put the blade down the throat just behind the head and draw it across with the point touching the bone. This cuts the jugular vein. Let the bird bleed a few seconds. Then put the point of knife and cutting edge against the roof of the mouth and force it into the brain cavity. Give a slight turn, severing the spinal cord. This releases control of the feathers, and some may be almost brushed off if done at once. This method is varied a little by some, but there are always two essentials; first to cut the jugular vein and next pierce the brain, paralyzing the nervous system. The work is done very quickly when one understands it. Of course it is necessary to study out these details very carefully before attempting to kill a bird. Dry picking is preferable for most markets, but the feathers do not always loosen in the way described, and then it is necessary to scald. Scalded poultry will sell about as well if the skin is not torn and the birds are "plumped." This consists in dipping them in hot water for a few seconds after picking and then at once into cold water, where they remain about 20 minutes. Roughly picked or bruised poultry is always discounted, so it pays to handle the birds carefully before killing, and to take off the feathers neatly. All animal heat must be removed before packing. This takes longer than is generally supposed, and neglect of it causes loss every year, when poultry known to be properly bled and only a short time on the road arrives at market in spoiled condition.

Methods of working up a retail egg trade are described elsewhere in this book. For the general wholesale market the 30-dozen case is the standard package. Where one is near market these cases may be made heavy enough to use many times, but for long-distance shipments, where the expense of returning is too great, the crates are made of cheap material and go with the eggs. The eggs are separated by pasteboard partitions, which may be bought in quantity of any dealer in poultry supplies. Very large quantities of eggs come to New York from the Middle West and Southwest. As might be expected, those from the southerly sections usually sell lowest, heat damage during the collection of carloads being greater in the warmer latitudes. Eggs are graded as fancy, choice, good, fair, inferior, checks and dirties. Fancy eggs should be strictly fresh, and not more than a week old when sold, but what they should be and what they are do not always tally. The quality of the other grades is suggested by their names. Checks are slightly cracked eggs that are sorted out, crated by themselves, and sold for immediate use.

Cold storage is the balance wheel of the egg and poultry trade, keeping it going at a comparatively even gait the year around, preventing the scarcity which causes prohibitive prices to all but the wealthy, and the glutted market, with figures below cost of production. The range of prices for a year will still show very high figures, such as 60 cents a dozen for new-laid eggs and 35 cents for fresh-killed poultry, yet there is no time when both eggs and poultry from storage, not fresh, but palatable and wholesome, may not be had at prices within reach of almost anyone. The scope of refrigeration has been much enlarged by dry air processes, which have made it possible to handle products that get musty under the dampness of ordinary ice storage. There are still many losses from improper handling, but good eggs properly stored may be kept for a full year.

CHAPTER XV.

Marketing Eggs.

The easiest money to be made in the poultry business is in marketing the products. A successful poultryman must be a good salesman. The extra money that may be secured by selling eggs to a special trade at an advanced price is almost clear gain. It should be 25 to 30 per cent additional above the profit in selling at the highest wholesale price. The margin will vary from one cent per dozen in small towns to five to 10 cents per dozen in large cities. It is not an easy matter to secure this high-class trade. Like everything else worth while, it requires years of effort and painstaking care. A poultryman must grow into his trade. High price is simply the premium paid for confidence in the goods. It is a just reward for a good reputation. Any neat and careful poultryman, however, should find no difficulty in raising his price two cents per dozen above the highest market in his neighborhood. As his customers become educated up to good eggs the price can be increased. The first essential in working up a special market is the ability to produce and deliver the goods. To do this three things are absolutely necessary; good eggs, an attractive package and regular delivery every week in the year. One is just as important as the other.

GOOD EGGS.—There is a great difference in eggs. They must, first of all, be new laid, that is to say, not over one week old. If they are gathered regularly each day and placed in a cool, dry room, they should suit the requirements of the most delicate taste. Daily or twice a week shipments are unnecessary with a private family trade, and would greatly increase the labor of handling and keeping of accounts as well as multiplying express charges. On the whole "eggs is eggs" when they go to or leave the average country store. A good farmer's good egg sells for no more than the poor farmer's poor egg when they once get into the class of ordinary "store-gathered" eggs, because they are in bad company. It is a positive injustice to the hens that laid the eggs, to the man who grew the grain to produce them, and to the one who gathers them thus to sell good eggs for the lowest possible price. The element of uncertainty as to just what is covered by the egg shell exaggerates the real difference and magnifies the premium paid for guaranteed quality. In other words, people are willing to pay an extra price rather than take any chances. Eggs are bought and sold largely "under sight and under seen" in the general market. While the general quality of market eggs has considerably increased in some respects of late years, due to the systematic handling of eggs by large dealers, the feature of age, which has much to do with quality, remains the same.

The eggs should be of large size. The customer who pays a good price is entitled to eggs that weigh not less than two ounces each. Eggs under two ounces should be sold to a special customer at a somewhat reduced rate. Small or medium eggs always suffer by contrast with large ones, but when placed in a crate by themselves they always show off to better advantage, and as they have the same quality of freshness and neatness as the other eggs they should command a premium above the general market. Good eggs should also be uniform in color, and the color should suit the fancy of the customer. The New York City market requires a pure white egg. Boston has a decided preference for a dark brown egg. Other things being equal, a difference of at least two cents per dozen will be paid just on account of color in these and other markets. It is a common practice now to assort and ship eggs according to the color requirements of the respective markets. Uniformity of grade counts for as much in selling eggs as it does in marketing fruit. One would not expect to ship red, green and russet apples of large, medium and small size in the same barrel. Yet it is a rule, not an exception, to find all kinds of eggs, big ones and litttle ones, long ones and round ones, eggs with brown, white, speckled or cream-colored shells in the same crate when they leave the farm. The very fact that they are mixed in colors and sizes brands them as "common eggs" in the eyes of the purchaser. They give the impression of not having come from any particular place or any special breed, but from anywhere and everywhere; just "picked up" eggs. This is a serious handicap. In order to produce the highest priced eggs one must keep purebred fowls, not because their eggs are any better to eat, but because they are better to look at.

Cleanliness is a necessity in selling fancy eggs. A dirty egg is a disgrace. It may be fresh, but no one will believe it. There are many degrees of cleanliness; spotless clean, clean, tolerably clean and dirty. Eggs as they come from the nest are usually tolerably clean. They are never spotless clean until each egg has been carefully inspected and the faintest trace of stain or dirt removed. Much can be done to keep eggs from becoming soiled which will save a large amount of labor. Dirty henhouses and yards cause dirty feet, which make dirty eggs. Clean nests will help to keep the eggs clean. Bright oat straw is one of the most desirable nest materials. Sawdust or clover hay and some other materials are apt to stain the shells. When cleaning eggs, both dry and damp cloths should be at hand. Sapolio is good to scour off a stain. A little sal soda in water will remove dirt more quickly. Vinegar and water will do the same thing. One should use as little water as possible. Washed eggs lose their natural finish and will not keep as well. Very dirty eggs, however, should be put to soak. All eggs should be perfectly dry when placed in the crates, and covered so that dust cannot settle on them. This cleaning operation is not expensive when done systematically. We pay under contract one cent per dozen for grading, cleaning and packing all of our eggs, both for market and for hatching. The person who does the work makes good wages.

The quality of fancy eggs must be good as to flavor, firmness of white and color of yolk. Care therefore must be taken in the feeding of fowls to have plenty of green food and a certain amount of corn, both of which give to the dull yolks a deep yellow color. Very pale yolks, which are certain to follow prolonged feeding without the foods mentioned, are apt to be looked upon with suspicion by particular customers. It is true that excessive feeding of laying hens upon foods which have a very pungent odor, such as onions or cabbage, will affect the flavor of the egg. Both turnips and cabbage, however, can be fed with perfect safety in limited quantities, especially if fowls are well supplied with other foods.

THE PACKAGE.—A good article is worthy of a neat package. Appearances count

FIG. 45. MAKING EGG CRATES.

for much in catching the eye or pleasing the palate. If eggs go to market in a neatly made, well varnished, carefully stenciled crate the customer has reason to expect that the same care used in packing the eggs has been exercised in producing and gathering them, and in this he usually is not mistaken. Good serviceable egg crates can be made with very slight expense. Most farmers should be able to make them. It is the most profitable kind of rainy day work. Fig. 45 shows a group of Cornell University poultry students making egg crates, which are used to deliver eggs from the College poultry plant. These crates have a capacity of multiples of three dozen; to hold either three dozen, six dozen, nine dozen, 12 dozen, 15 dozen or 30 dozen. Regular commercial egg crates are purchased for five to ten cents each with fillers. The best ends are used to form the ends of the new crates of various sizes. Three-eighths-inch Georgia pine ceiling is used for sides and top, which is nailed with two-inch finishing nails. The bottoms are made from the best of the material taken from the sides of the old egg crates. Narrow cleats are placed on the sides for handles, and upon the top of the cover to make it solid. Two three-inch strap hinges and a hasp are placed on the cover. The whole box is then sandpapered if necessary, covered with hard oil finish, which makes a much neater looking package, easier to keep clean than one which is painted. The name of the farm or of the proprietor, with the home address and the products shipped, should then be stencilled on the top of the package, also upon the sides where room will permit. The Cornell stencil is in two parts. With the first part a large white egg, 10 inches long, is painted upon the box. When this is dry another stencil is used to print the words, "Cornell University, College of Agriculture, Poultry Products, Ithaca, N. Y. Quality Guaranteed." A neat stencil on any package is a splendid advertisement, and makes the chances of loss of crates in transit very much less. As a finishing touch we purchase little brass padlocks, with duplicate keys. They cost 12½ cents each and they are money makers, not so much because they prevent stealing eggs, but because the wealthy customer is willing to pay a cent or more a dozen just for the sake of having his neighbor see that he gets eggs direct from the farm by express each week with a padlock on the box. Our experience in working up a large private family trade in and about New York City is that the best advertiser is a pleased customer. To illustrate, we have one family that has purchased eggs from us for many years. They referred a friend to us, who became a regular customer, who in turn wanted us to send eggs to another friend. Another string of customers started by a wealthy man visiting the farm and finding us packing eggs for the private family trade. He asked why he could not have eggs sent to him also. He is one of our best customers at the present time, and through his friendship four others have been secured. Farmers who take Summer boarders, or those who sell produce to Summer hotels, have excellent opportunities for finding city customers for eggs. The private family trade, however, is not without its disadvantages. One of these is that there are a multitude of details in looking after a large number of comparatively small shipments ranging from six to 15 dozen. This makes a good deal of bookkeeping. Families are apt to leave the city at certain times during the year which necessarily interrupts the general output of eggs. However, some of our customers continue to have eggs shipped to their Summer resort, where they are willing to pay double express charges. The most serious difficulties have been the breakage by express companies. Occasionally they make good the loss, after much correspondence and delay.

REGULARITY OF SHIPMENT.—The people who pay high prices want their eggs on time, rain or shine. They usually want the same number per week the year round. One's capacity, therefore, to cater to this trade is somewhat measured by the number of eggs which he can produce during the months of greatest scarcity, namely October, November and December. We find, however, that our customers are very obliging, and stay with us over these periods with a somewhat diminished supply. In order to discourage excessive egg eating during the period of scarcity, we make our prices according to the law of supply and demand. While our prices are not as high perhaps as some are getting, we are quite well pleased with the results, but we are always looking for higher prices. Our scale of prices is 25 cents per dozen for April, May, June and July; 35 cents for August and September; 40 cents for October and November; 45 for December and January; 35 February and March. The customer in every case pays the express charges and returns the empty box. We found that there was less trouble from breakage where the customer who was on the spot was personally responsible for settling with the express company for damage. These prices, therefore, net us about seven to eight cents per dozen by the year more than the highest wholesale market quotation for fancy nearby white eggs. During the Spring months, when most eggs are laid, a large trade in eggs for hatching takes care of most of the surplus. At the end of a hatching season the Summer hotel trade will handle any surplus which we may have at about 25 cents per dozen. Whatever the system of marketing, the problem of regularity of supply throughout the year is the hardest one to meet, and in a measure it remains unsolved. With the best of care one cannot expect to get more than 10 to 15 eggs per day per 100 hens in large numbers during the months of October, November and December and not over 20 or 30 per cent from early-hatched pullets. It is true that individual flocks should do much better than this for a time, but if there are many flocks, some of the others will not be laying as well. Even with the high price to be secured for eggs during the late Fall and early Winter months, the net profits will be less than at any other season of the year, but it does not follow that we should only produce eggs during the regular laying season. It will most likely be found that the flocks that have laid the most eggs during the Winter will also produce best during the rest of the year. If hens do not lay during the Winter they are a dead loss, which must be made up out of the Summer profits. Unfortunately when a hen stops laying she doesn't stop eating. A more potent argument still is that one cannot secure a satisfactory market for Spring and Summer eggs only. Many customers pay high prices in Summer simply to hang on to their supply for the Winter.

CHAPTER XVI.

Companions of the Hen.

THE GUINEA FOWL.—There are two varieties of Guineas, Pearl and White. There is no difference in their characteristics save in their color. The Pearl variety should be bluish-gray in color, each feather covered with white spots resembling pearls, hence its name. It should be free from any white feathers in any part of the plumage. The neck is covered with black hairs near the head, and between that and the feathers is a soft down, of a light brown color, that glistens in the sun. On the top of the head is a horny spike that turns backward. The bill and legs are brown. The white variety should be a pure white in plumage, with a yellow orange or yellowish-white bill and legs, this being the only difference between them and the Pearl variety. Some birds of the Pearl variety have white feathers in the breast and wings, but are mongrels, being a cross between the two varieties. They are great foragers, and will pick up enough bugs and injurious insects more than to pay for themselves. They do not stand confinement well, and will not lay more than one-half as many eggs as if allowed to run at large. If fed regularly morning and night they will always be on hand for their share. They desire to roost in trees near the barn at night, and are most excellent guards either night or day; anything out of the usual astir, they will set up a great cry. They roost so high that they are out of the way of thieves or wild animals. In their wild state they will fight and drive other fowls, but if used kindly as other poultry, they will stay and feed with other fowls without showing much of this pugnacious habit. The Guinea hen is a Spring and Summer layer, and lays from 90 to 120 eggs yearly. They like a secluded place to lay in. When their nests are found, leave two or three eggs, or they will leave the nest for another place. Better set their eggs under hens to hatch, as the Guinea does not sit until too late in this latitude to have the young get grown before Winter. Besides, if raised by common hens, they can be taken care of better, for they must be fed often, as the young eat but little at a time. Fifteen to 17 eggs can be set under a good-sized hen, and with good care all can be raised. Their eggs are small, but make up in quality what is lost in size. Their meat is excellent, and has a gamy flavor. The cocks can be distinguished by their screeching noise, also by the spike on their heads being larger, and by holding their heads higher. Their ear tubes are larger, and generally curl in a sort of semi-circle toward the beak. The hens make a noise that sounds like "too quick," and seldom screech.

PIGEONS AND SQUABS.—J. E. Stevenson says: Almost any dry and fairly warm room may be fixed to answer nicely for pigeons. Essentials are convenience of attendant, a good roof, no holes or cracks in sides, and above all strictly rat-proof, as if rats get a taste of your squabs, they will do more damage than any one thing I can think of. Allow about 250 square feet of floor space for each 50 pairs of breeders.

Nest boxes should be arranged convenient for the attendant. Suitable boxes may usually be obtained cheaply at your grocer's; select boxes from eight to 12 inches square. Nail a board three or four inches wide across the front to keep eggs or small squabs from falling out. Bore a hole in back near top and hang on nails driven in the walls. These may be quickly taken down, cleaned and hung up again. There should be two nest boxes for each pair of breeders, as often a good pair of breeders will have a new nest and eggs in one box before their squabs are ready to leave the other. It is best to hang the boxes in pairs close together, and each pair of boxes far enough from the next, so that the occupants can't stand in their doorway, or on their house top and fight with their neighbor.

Put in windows enough for light and ventilation in warm weather, but don't worry about ventilation in cold weather; the problem then is how to shut it out, as it is almost impossible to get a building closed too closely in cold weather, unless overcrowded with stock.

The fly should contain about twice the amount of ground space as the building, and may be made from two-inch poultry mesh netting, but when sparrows are numerous it will pay to use one-inch mesh netting, so as to exclude them from the fly. I use netting four feet wide and wire together with pig rings. If the soil is not sandy or gravelly, the ground in fly should be covered with three or four inches of sand and this renewed occasionally, so that it will always be in good shape to feed the birds on.

Homers are unquestionably the best all-round breeders, and if they have good food and care will produce first-class squabs, and lots of them. Unless you can get good mated breeders, not over three or four years old, I think it better to get youngsters from the nests when about four or five weeks old, or ready for market, and raise your own breeders. It will be six months before you begin to see any profit, but you have the advantage of knowing the age of your birds, and that they are good for eight or 10 years' service.

It is best to start with no more than you can familiarize yourself with and be able to tell which are mates, keeping the unmated birds separate from those that are mated. You can mate almost any cock and hen you wish mated together by placing them in a coop by themselves a few days, and when once mated they are usually there for life unless forcibly separated. When it is convenient to do so it is best to get the young birds from two different breeders, and in mating use one from each breeder for each pair, so as to have no possibility of inbreeding.

For feed use coarse cracked corn three parts, whole corn two parts, wheat two parts, Canada peas two parts, hemp seed one part. Always be sure that the feed is sweet and sound, and never feed any new grain until it is well dried out and hard. When convenient I prefer feeding three times per day on the ground in the fly, giving them all they will clean up; if not convenient to feed at noon, cracked corn may be kept before them all the time in a feeder so arranged that it will be kept clean and dry. Always give fresh water when feeding, and have a pan of water large enough for them to bathe in.

Keep good sharp grit and ground oyster shells before them all the time. Also keep a mixture of ground charcoal six parts, old mortar or plaster three parts and fine salt one part, where they may have free access to it, and supply them with tobacco stems for them to make their nests with. These may be either on the floor of the house or in the fly, and the birds will use them as they need them. Any coarse hay or straw will answer in place of the tobacco, but the tobacco is a protection against lice. The squabs are ready for market when four to five weeks old, and first-class squabs bring from $3 to $4.50 per dozen in New York markets, according to the season. If you get good breeding stock and give them good care they will repay you well.

CARE OF TURKEYS.—We have found young turkeys as easy to raise as chickens when cared for in the following manner: The method of hatching is immaterial—a reliable incubator, hens or turkey hens, whichever is most convenient. The time, however, is important. As the Springs here are cold and often wet we find it better to have poults hatch about June 1. Have sufficient turkey hens sitting to care for the poults when hatched. If they have been sitting but a week you may put the newly-hatched, but thoroughly dried, little poults under them at night and they will care for them. Never try to raise turkeys in a brooder or with common hens. Do not give more than 20 poults to each hen to mother, and place turkey and brood in a triangular pen made of boards 12 inches wide and placed on edge. Place within this enclosure a house of some kind. If the weather be warm an A-shaped lath coop will answer. Have the pen movable, and move to fresh grass frequently. Feed the turkey plenty of corn, but do not feed the poults until 36 hours after the last one is hatched. Provide fresh water in clean drinking fountains and grit.

Sprinkle the hen with a good insect powder, and keep the poults at all times free from lice. Between the third and sixth day spread the wing of each little poult and pull out the six quills you will find starting to grow along the outer edge. When the poults can fly over this pen let them have free range with their mother, but see that they come home at night if you are obliged to bring them a few times. Feed liberally when they come home, and always have grit and fresh water where they may have free access to it. Keep their house and pen clean. A turkey will not live in filthy quarters, nor if lousy. If you are making a success of the dry-feeding system with chicks you will succeed with the turkeys by the same system. Pinhead or flake oatmeal, dry bread soaked with milk or water and squeezed dry, curds mixed with chopped onion or dandelion tops are all good foods. Sometimes we are able to buy through our grocer breakfast food or pinhead oatmeal that has become wormy (not musty) at greatly reduced prices, and they make excellent food for turkeys or chicks. Feed no sloppy foods and not too much at one time.

BANTAM BREEDING.—Bantams need but little room, and little feed. They are very attractive and useful, not merely pets, as they are good layers of good-sized and rich eggs. I have used an incubator for hatching, but prefer hens. If I have Bantams that I can spare I use them, but usually common hens. If large hens are used their nests should be in a low box six inches deep, the nest made but little dishing, as the eggs will move more readily as the hen steps among them. For this reason the fewer eggs under a hen the better. The eggs are quite as likely to be fertile and hatch as any larger breeds. A box should be placed over the hen after she has been fed and watered each day. This not only secures her from being disturbed, but prevents her from coming off many times a day, as some will, each time endangering the eggs. I do not find the chicks quite as hardy or as easy to raise as larger breeds until feathered. They feather so young and fast that they need good feed and care at this time. For a few days when first hatched, hard-boiled eggs and bread crumbs chopped fine are best for them; later cracked wheat, millet and ground beef scraps, and some whole grain. For head and throat lice and around the little cluster of feathers in front of the vent use a little grease. Fresh butter is good; sweet cream is still better, and will not injure if used liberally on turkeys or chickens. This will do little good, however, if the hen has lice. This season I have taken a feather, and with a liquid lice killer touched the hen under and above in many places. If this is done in the morning when the chicks are a few days old, and the hen in an open coop, so the chicks can get plenty of air, it will not hurt them, but will rid both hen and chicks of lice for a long time; if not for the season.

THE DUCK.—The principal breeds are Pekin, Rouen, Cayuga, Muscovy and Aylesbury. The Pekin is most extensively raised. The following are the methods of a successful commercial breeder. For the first four days after hatching they have a mixture of two-thirds bread crumbs and boiled eggs, in the proportion of four parts of bread to one of egg, and one-third rolled oats. At the end of four days five per cent of sand, not gravel, is added to the food, and each day following, until the end of the first week, the food is gradually changed by substituting bran and meal for egg and bread. After a week two parts of wheat bran, one of cornmeal and 10 per cent of beef scrap are given, and the five per cent sand is continued until the ducks are fattened. Salt is used for flavoring at all times. About the time sand is given green food is begun. This must be tender and succulent on the start, like clover, green rye or tender grass cut fine. In Winter cabbage, turnips, beets, potatoes or any vegetables chopped into small pieces with a root cutter, or even nice clover hay cut and cooked will do. The green stuff is mixed with the other food in a large box, and moistened, but not made sloppy. At seven weeks old fattening commences, using two parts cornmeal to one of bran, and 15 per cent beef scrap, fed four times a day, all they will eat up clean. At 10 weeks they weigh not far from five pounds and are then marketed. At that time the temporary plumage is perfected. If allowed to go longer the pin feathers of the adult plumage begin to start, and it would be six weeks before they would again be in condition. The ducks to be fattened are not allowed to go into the water, as the exercise works off their flesh. Those kept as breeders swim all they wish. They are selected when five weeks old, and never fattened. Their feed is one-third each of bran, vegetables and corn and oats, with a little animal feed in the form of beef scrap, fish scrap and fresh fish.

In marketing, the desired number are removed from the pen and driven to another enclosure. There they find a bath with pure running water. This being their first opportunity for bathing, they go at it at once and soon come out clean and white. Then they go to the slaughter house, where they are killed and picked in the usual way.

Ducks cannot stand the sun, so their yard should be well shaded. Plum trees make an excellent shade, and usually thrive in a poultry yard. Another essential is plenty of pure water for drinking, so arranged that they cannot get into it. Where one has water under pressure small streams may be piped into little troughs and kept running steadily.

CHAPTER XVII.

The Health of the Hen.

IMPORTANCE OF PREVENTION.—Vermin, germs and improper care are responsible for most poultry diseases. Yet when the conditions favoring sanitary care of the flock are understood probably no other animal can be more safely raised in large numbers. The slight value of the individual fowl makes the employment of a veterinarian out of the question; most that he can do is to advise as to stamping out disease and preventing future outbreaks. It is sometimes claimed that successful doctoring can be done at long range and at a considerable lapse of time, but the bodies of fowls are as delicate and complex as those of other animals, and immediate attention and nursing are needed. Ideally the poultryman should so care for the flock that it could not have disease. The remedies of the poultryman are not quinine, calomel and aconite, but the axe, the fence and quick lime or other disinfectants judiciously used.

HEREDITY.—Hereditary diseases among fowls are few. Probably the most important is lack of vitality inherited by young chicks as a result of too close inbreeding of the parents, or the fact that either parent is too fat. Inherited weaknesses, the result of inbreeding, cannot be cured. The poultryman must either begin with new stock or replace some portion of it with new blood, and so breed out the weakness. Very close inbreeding may result in deformed bodies, wings or feet, in deranged nervous systems, or in sterility. On the other hand, advocates of line breeding have secured good results while trying to avoid the faults of very close inbreeding.

CORRECT FEEDING.—Improper feeding with the usual foodstuffs does not cause many diseases, but it may cause loss in the productivity of the underfed or overfed individual. Starvation and obesity approach diseased conditions as extremes are reached. Overfeeding is attended by the most serious difficulties. The fat being deposited to excess in various organs as the liver, heart or oviduct muscles weakens them and often ends in the destruction of the fowl. Ruptures of the liver and various veins of the body seem to be brought about by fatty degeneration; also a failure of muscular power to extrude the egg. Clean, uncontaminated water aids in dissolving the food, and grit, to assist in grinding it, should always be at hand. While it is possible that chickens may survive some time without grit it is certain that they grow much better and keep healthier when it is at hand. The diagnosis of disorders from incorrect feeding is difficult. The scales should soon tell whether the fowls are too heavy, even if the caretaker has not discovered when handling them on the roost that their flesh is too fat or flabby, or possibly too bony. The condition of the fowl must be noted by the sense of feeling as well as by the eye. The only means of restoring too fat fowls to a normal condition is to deprive them of a portion of the food they would otherwise need and make them hunt and pick for what they get. Starve them into health.

"COLDS" OR INFLUENZA are caused by abrupt changes of temperature. They may occur in Winter or Summer, but are always the result of a draft. In an endeavor to secure more air to carry off odors houses have been arranged so that drafts blew directly upon the fowls. A cold is indicated by sneezing and a slight discharge at the nostrils which collect dirt and straws. If severe cases the affected fowls droop. In an outbreak of this character there may be inflammation of the lungs. The only remedy for colds is to arrange the house so that there can be no cross drafts from doors, windows or cracks. The use of muslin curtains instead of some of the glass windows is a preventive. These act by permitting the moisture transpired by the hens to pass though, by retaining heat, stopping direct drafts and allowing slow diffusion of the inside and outside air. Frozen combs, wattles and feet are prevented by keeping the sleeping chamber as dry as possible and comfortably warm. This is effected by muslin curtains which divide the roosting place from the rest of the room, and limit the space to be heated by the fowls.

SANITARY HOUSES.—Moisture in the henhouse should be avoided, as it is most destructive to the comfort and health of the fowl. The only economical method of doing this is by permitting the inside air to exchange its moisture contents freely with the outside. The muslin screen seems at present to be the cheapest and best. Many poultrymen make use of the loft of the larger houses for ventilation by covering a loose flooring with a foot of hay and opening doors in the gables. All inside structures should be made so that fowls cannot injure themselves. The lighter breeds usually suffer little harm from bruises, but the heavier may receive them on their feet or their wings on account of the construction of the house. As a rule the dropping board and perch should be well upon the side of the house, so that the hens will have all the floor space and the roosts will be in the warmer part of the building. For the heavier breeds runways should be made leading up to the roosts and the roost wired in with removable netting, so that the birds cannot fly down. Their wings are as compared to their body weight so weak that in the short distance from roost to floor they receive little help from them and fall instead of fly. This applies to the heavier American breeds as well as the Asiatic. The wings often get bruised by trying to fly through too small openings when scared or by careless handling. Fowls contract but few diseases from the yards aside from the parasitic. They are more liable to the effects of improper feeding and the lack of exercise when confined, but when once they are yarded the poultryman is compelled to supply the feed, water and means of exercise in order to realize his profit. As compared to free range the discomforts of the ordinary henyard are many. Too frequently no provision is made for protection of the fowls from the cold Winter blasts or fiercely hot Summer sun, against which the fowl when allowed free range always chooses sheltered thickets or the lee of some fence, wall or building. The chief protection against vermin, parasites and communicable diseases is the wire fence.

WIRE FENCE.—The height chosen should be according to the fowls kept and the size of the yards. For small yards those 40 or 50 feet wide by 80 or 100 long, a height of seven feet for Leghorns, is ample; three feet of woven wire, one inch mesh, is used at the bottom and buried at least six inches in the soil. Four feet of two-inch mesh fills the top. The corner posts are set like the others, whether in dug holes or driven. A stiff pole for a brace is placed horizontally between the corner and next post, provided the latter is not more than eight or 10 feet away, and at a height of four feet from the ground. Notches may be made to hold the brace in position or it may be nailed. A No. 9 wire is then passed around the bottom of the corner post and top of the second post and back to the corner post, where after pulling as tight as possible the ends are fastened. Nails may be used to keep the wire in place while fastening. A short iron rod should then be used to twist the wire by placing it between the two strands near the middle and turning it over and over until the twisted wire is taut. This completes a corner that will not give and will be heaved by freezing very little. If displaced it may be easily driven back. The gates are made four feet wide with a removable foot-wide board across the bottom. These can be cheaply made of furring two inches wide, a few nails and woven wire. Cut four pieces the width of the gate. Cut two the length of the gate. Cut one to reach from the bottom next the hinge to the top on the swinging side and miter its corners so that they fit against the side sticks, especially at the bottom. When fastened together a space is left between the top and bottom cross-pieces. The nails driven through the three pieces and the cross brace together with the separated double pieces make a very strong light gate. The advantage of this fence is that fowls do not try to dig under. They rarely try to fly over. Only cats and hawks can enter. The fence seems to be practically rat proof. The tendency of animals to tunnel under seems to be avoided by the clear view through the wire. Dogs, skunks and minks are surely kept out. No communicable disease can enter excepting when carried by some hen or by the attendant. The disease that is carried through the air is very rare. Even mites and hen lice are little likely to leave their haunts to invade other pens.

TREATMENT OF YARDS.—Manure from healthy fowls will so pollute small yards as to make them unhealthy and render cultivation of the soil necessary. It is not likely that even disease germs would outlast the attacks of the soil bacteria throughout a season when the ground is properly spaded or plowed and cultivated. The uncleaned hen roost has been called the greatest meance to the hens, but probably the yards and the water furnish the larger part of the infection. Yards which are virtually fields and can be cultivated for various crops in succession furnish the best facilities for the hen and are the healthiest. By locating the houses at the touching corners of four fields the fences can easily be arranged so as to use either at will. The portable house has its sanitary value in the warm months. The turning under of polluted soil and removal of the fowls during the cultivation of a crop renew the fields so that they can be used alternately year after year to the advantage of both crop and fowls. Newly hatched and small chicks must be yarded somewhat differently from old fowls. For these in Spring and Summer there is no better place than some spot within the orchard which has been enclosed by a three-foot inch mesh net wire fence, with lower edge buried in the ground. This will keep them from being lost in the wet grass.

BROODING TROUBLES.—The diseases of brooding are mainly those which arise from the lack of heat and food, the former by far the more important. The result of brooding by the hens is the application of heat to the chick, and when food is plenty the hen that is most successful is the one that has paid the strictest attention to business. So in artificial brooding success depends upon the application of heat. When disease occurs in hatching and brooding artificially it is in most cases directly due to the lack of heat or its improper application and not to the stock from which the eggs came. The success of artificial brooding will depend upon the brooder and its treatment. Artificially raised chicks being deprived of the hen's care learn but slowly and must be housed and yarded for some time. There need be no worry about chicks contracting such diseases as gapes if they are kept from other fowls and on uninfected runs. It is safer and more economical of labor to brood the chicks until they are four or five weeks old even in Summer.

ROUP.—Bacterial diseases which show their main symptoms in the head are known as roup, the nostrils become stopped by inflammation and inflammatory products, the mucous sacs of the eye socket become filled and often cause the head to swell and the eye to project. An examination of the nasal opening in the roof of the mouth often shows a yellow cheesy deposit. These discharges have a characteristic odor of dead tissue. The cheesy deposits also extend to the opening of the windpipe. When the breathing becomes obstructed the fowl emits a gasping noise which gives rise to the name roup. It is probable that there are no less than three, perhaps four, distinct diseases which are all called roup. To the poultryman this fact has at present but little importance, as the same means are taken in combating each. While the main symptom exists in the head the more severe forms involve the whole body. These diseases are readily diagnosed by general droopiness, by visible inflammation of the head, by roupy sounds and the odor. They are all caused by organisms which pass from bird to bird. They begin by the introduction of a fowl carrying the disease into the flock and their spread is greatly favored by conditions which cause the fowls to catch cold. To avoid the disease one should thoroughly examine the heads of each new purchase and keep all the fowls separate from other flocks. The houses should be so constructed as to avoid direct drafts on the hens, and neither be too moist nor too hot. Fowls kept in cold sheds rarely take cold. When the fowls have once contracted either of the roup diseases there is no medicinal remedy that will be satisfactory or that it will pay to give. An affected flock should be at once quarantined in a light, dry room with floor and without direct drafts. The room should be whitewashed thoroughly in all parts, including floor. The floor should be sanded, but during the virulence of the outbreak straw should be omitted. The hens should be fed sparingly so as not to fatten too greatly during their quarantine. While medicine as iron sulphate, carbonate or disinfectants, as often recommended, may be put into the drinking water, the quantity advised is hardly ever sufficient to make the water antiseptic. It is better to scald out the dishes regularly and give pure drinking water. By remodelling or changing the quarantine quarters and confinement on the board floor most of the fowls will get better. Some may get worse and these it will be necessary to kill. There is little use for disinfectants beyond the whitewash, which should be used quite liberally each time the house is cleaned. If made thin a liberal amount spread on the floor after sweeping up the sand will quite thoroughly disinfect. The whitewash should for this purpose be freshly made from unslaked lime. If one preferred, any of the coal tar disinfectants could be used. Whitewash is cheap and efficient for all purposes when thoroughly applied. It would not be wise to allow a flock that had once been affected with roup ever to have complete liberty again for fear of a future outbreak from some undiscovered patient. They should be kept securely yarded and housed. After they have become sufficiently aged and all the eggs for hatching be obtained from them that are needed, they should be killed, quarters thoroughly disinfected and their yards abandoned for a time to allow disinfection through changes of the weather. This may be aided by liming and cultivation.

DIPHTHERETIC ROUP.—Fowls with diphtheretic roup have been treated by swabbing out the membranes and touching them with peroxide of hydrogen, two per cent carbolic acid solution, borax and other more or less imperfect disinfecting preparations. These often succeed. While diphtheretic roup in fowls seems from recent investigation to be an entirely different disease from diphtheria in man, the operator should take no chances and disinfect his hands and operating-tools in two per cent carbolic acid solution after a thorough scrubbing in soap and water. Above all, should there be no carrying of buckets, brooms or hoes from the quarantine hospital to other houses. It is better to provide a pair of rubbers for use in the quarantine house and yard so as to prevent tracking infection from house to house.

CHOLERA.—The cholera type of diseases, or those in which the germs enter the system through the intestinal tract and are disseminated through the droppings, comprise three diseases perhaps more, all due to different germs. They should be handled when an outbreak occurs much the same as the roup diseases. However, in these diseases, especially the typhoidal forms, there is more danger from infection contaminating the ground, and great care should be taken with infected ground either by abandonment or by intensive cultivation. Liming when necessary to correct acidity, spading and cultivation will enable the nitrifying bacteria to grow which in warm seasons will destroy the disease making germs. The author has frequently collected infected fowls carried them for some miles placed them in a coop with board floor, believing that they would die only to have them improve under the changed surroundings. Little is known about the length of time either of this class of diseases may live in the ground or in the animal. If remedies are given it should be remembered that any alkalies as carbonate of soda, Epson or Glauber salts create inflammation of the intestine and permit germs to enter the system more readily. The acid stops diarrhœas when present and may possibly be helpful. The presence of the virulent communicable disease of the cholera type is ascertained by droopiness of the fowls and subsequent death. Oftentimes the droopiness passes unobserved. Diseases produced by errors of feeding generally take some time to develop unless something acting like a poison is taken, and then a large number are suddenly taken; some die and the others recover. The various forms of this class of disease cannot easily be told apart in the hen yard. One of them, infectious leukæmia, causes death within three or four days, with scarcely 12 hours droopiness and without any easily ascertainable symptoms. Fowl cholera lasts from two to three weeks, is accompanied by droopiness and may or may not be accompanied by diarrhœa. Diarrhœa in fowls is indicated by frequent evacautations of soft greenish, brownish or yellowish stools. The white watery stool sometimes seen is not indicative of diarrhœa, but of lack of intestinal evacuations. It consists of the lime products secreted by the kidneys and is usually in excess in fevers. The disease called "going light" in fowls may arise from chronic forms of cholera, from starvation produced by mechanical derangements of the system or possibly from bacterial and parasitic forms. As the name indicates the fowls become thin and light in weight. When communicable disease is concerned there will be no attempt at diagnosis until the fowls are visibly affected and begin to die. Should they die suddenly without previous illness one may suspect infectious leukæmia. Should there be some droopiness noted and the fowls stop feeding cholera may be the cause. In both these diseases many fowls of the flock will be affected, while in chronic forms of these and other diseases there will be but few at a time. Since medicinal treatment will always prove unsatisfactory the exact diagnosis of a disease will not matter, for the same thorough steps must be taken to limit the spread of the disease whether it be one thing or another. There is no help for the poultryman except in that perpetual vigilance which wards off all diseases.

GAPES.—This is caused by worms one-half to three-fourths inch long, which attach themselves inside the windpipe. They are always red from the blood taken from the fowls. Here they breed and when adult are coughed out upon the ground, when their eggs are sown broadcast. Artificially raised chicks will not contract gape worms unless placed on the ground where chickens have contracted or scattered the disease. Earth worms may carry the trouble. Gape worms are indicated by the frequent gaping or gasping of the chicks for air. The old familiar horse hair loop or the feather end dipped in turpentine will remove them. However, time and chicks may be saved during the succeeding year by removing the coops to a new lot, cultivating the old place and keeping the chicks from it. The time required for land to disinfect itself of gape worms is not known. Since robins and other birds may perpetuate them it is possible that a given space may never be exactly safe. Some poultrymen by keeping the chicks on a board floor for some time have avoided this trouble.

SCALY-LEG.—Another parasitic disease caused by minute mites which insert themselves under the scales covering the feet is called "scaly-leg." While not particularly noticeable in early stages it is readily diagnosed by the comparatively enormous roughening of the scales caused in the later stages. Since it does not spread from fowl to fowl it should be treated regularly until cured. The legs should be dipped in carbolized vaseline, sweet oil, kerosene or washed with creoline dips. The oils act better than water dips because they last on the legs longer, and thus draw out the mites. If the dips are repeated the scales soften and the inflammation disappears until feet that will seem beyond cure will again appear healthy and comparatively smooth.

SURGICAL TREATMENT.—Crop-bound is a condition in which the crop becomes packed with food because of stoppage of its outlet by coarse material. It is easily remedied by cutting into the crop at that part which is on top when the fowl stands. After emptying all its contents the raw edges should be treated with two per cent carbolic acid or creoline mixture. Then sew the crop by placing the raw edges together and tying each time the needle is passed through. Coarse linen or silk thread is equally good. Do not put the inside lining edges of the crop together, but the raw edges. Then disinfect again and sew the raw edges of the skin together. Give the hen water and feed a little soft feed for three days. Incisions into swellings and abscesses do little permanent good, for there is usually no cure effected. Blunting or removing the spurs of the cocks often saves the lives of others and keeps them from gashing the sides of the hens.

DOCTORING POULTRY.—The general rules for guarding the health of poultry, given above by Dr. Curtice, would, if followed out carefully, prevent any serious outbreak of disease. There would be few deaths in the flock except those from accident or old age. He does not advocate dosing or fussing with sick hens, and he is largely right, because when a hen becomes sick enough to make her condition evident she is often too far gone for medicine. For those who wish to doctor their hens we add a few simple rules of advice. Read the notes on Tonics for Poultry with care, and do not be too anxious to stuff the fowls with medicine. Good food and clean and comfortable quarters give a condition which no drugs can possibly supply.

Lice are responsible for many of the so-called poultry diseases. They weaken the hen's vitality and put her into a condition which makes it impossible for her to do well. A lousy hen may have ruffled feathers, a dark comb, looseness of the bowels and other symptoms which indicate some form of chicken cholera. What folly it would be to dose such a hen with medicines or "tonics" and leave the lice on her body or leave vermin in the henhouse which she occupies. Would it not be just as great folly to doctor a hen for roup, and spray her throat and then put her back into some damp and breezy house where other roupy hens stay? This will show the wisdom of what Dr. Curtice says and the need of proper care. If one wishes to try a "roup cure" on the nostrils or throat the following will be found as good as any: Equal parts ammonia, turpentine and glycerine. We have seen cases of roup that seemed to be relieved by dipping the entire head into kerosene. One ounce of chlorate of potash in a pint of water makes a good wash for cases of sore throat, but of course hens needing any such treatment should be put by themselves. Reports are made of successful treatment of cholera by giving in the early stages one teaspoonful of a solution of one ounce of hyposulphite of soda in a pint of water. Dry, unslaked lime is sometimes used to help chicks dispose of gape worms. The chicks are put into a covered box with a layer of lime at the bottom. The whole thing is shaken to stir up the lime into a dust. Do not leave the chicks inside over two minutes.

If combs are smeared with glycerine or vaseline they will not be so liable to frost bite. A good dressing for all wounds on animals is one part carbolic acid in three parts of sweet oil. Feather pulling is usually caused by idleness or a lack of meat in the diet. Generally there are a few birds in the flock who do most of the mischief. If they can be caught at it they would better be killed. Make the hens work or scratch for their food and provide meat in some form. Little chicks sometimes kill and eat each other. Members of a flock have been known to attack some wounded bird and pick it to pieces. The victim usually has some wound or sore that shows blood, and the others attack this spot. It usually indicates a lack of meat in the ration. This should be supplied, and if the trouble is bad the chicks should be separated, taken to fresh ground and sorted so that the smaller ones are kept separate.

THE CHICKEN MITE.—This little insect is probably the worst single enemy of the average farm hen. It does more damage than the large body lice, and is harder to destroy. No hen can be profitable when infested with these mites. The hen stops laying, the feathers are roughened, the head becomes pale, the bird is a picture of unthrift. It is not uncommon for hatching hens to die on the nest, or to be driven away from their eggs by these horrible creatures. The mites also attack the little chicks and kill great numbers of them. The insects work mostly at night, and not only suck the hen's blood but destroy her rest. The insect is very small and very active. Fig. 46 shows one greatly enlarged. In life they are one-twenty-fifth of an inch long, gray in color except when filled with blood, when they are red. They usually only remain upon the hen long enough to secure a meal. They hide in cracks or in filth and litter during the day, and at night when the hens return to the roosts crawl out and begin their blood-sucking. The eggs are laid and hatched in these hiding places. The under sides of the roosts, the litter and straw in the nests are favorite places. They breed rapidly, and unless destroyed will swarm all over the house. There is no doubt that these mites can be carried from one farm to another on poultry, coops, clothing or eggs bought for hatching. That is one reason why no strange fowl should be put in the house without a thorough dusting with insect powder. A good way to use the powder is to put it in a large pepper box and shake it out among the hen's feathers. In some cases hens are dipped in a warm tea, made by steeping tobacco stems, or a preparation like Zenoleum. The "dipped"

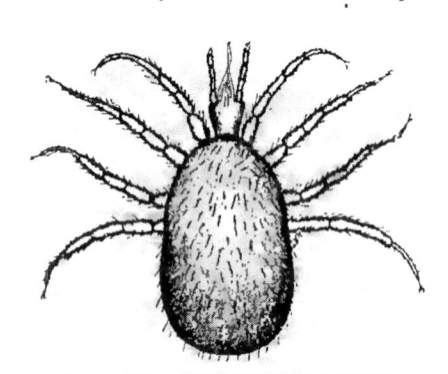

FIG. 46. CHICKEN MITE.

hen should be kept out of all draughts and kept in a warm, sunny place.

In clearing a house of mites, the litter and straw should be taken from the floor and nests and burned. The manure must be taken out. As the mites spend the day on the under side of the roosts they must be taken out and painted with kerosene and smeared with grease. There will still be millions of the insects left in cracks and holes. They can only be killed by thorough scrubbing and spraying with some biting liquid again and again until both insects and their eggs are destroyed. The two best sprays are named below. In houses where these mites are found all the fixtures should be loose so they can be taken out for cleaning. A form of nest used in Mississippi is shown in Fig. 47. This is well suited to a hot country. In this the pieces C. C. are the only ones fastened to the building. The whole thing can be easily removed for cleaning. The Mississippi Station recommends cleaning the house every two weeks, and then using a dust of three parts slacked lime and one part sulphur. This is thrown in the air up to the roof of the house until the whole place is filled with the dust.

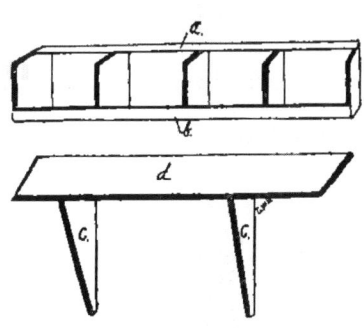

FIG. 47. SANITARY NEST

KEROSENE EMULSION.—This emulsion is better than pure kerosene, because it will dissolve in water and may be sprayed or washed over the walls. Take one-half pound of hard soap and shave it into a gallon of soft water; put it on the fire and bring it to a boil. By this time the soap will be dissolved. Then remove the soap solution from the fire and stir into it at once, while hot, two gallons of kerosene. This makes a thick, creamy emulsion, which is made ready for use by diluting with 10 volumes of soft water, and stirring well. Make up as much of the stock emulsion as it is thought will be needed. This can be kept in a suitable vessel and a portion taken out and diluted as needed. If the bucket or holder attached to the spray pump holds five gallons, one-half gallon of the stock emulsion should be taken and put into the bucket or holder and four and one-half gallons of soft water added, and the whole well stirred. It is then ready to be sprayed on the places occupied by the mites.

LIME AND SULPHUR WASH.—This is the wash recommended to fruit growers for spraying to kill the San José scale. Some fruit growers drive the spray pump right up to the henhouse door and thoroughly spray the inside. The wash is made in the proportion of 40 pounds of lime, 20 pounds of sulphur and five pounds of caustic soda in 60 gallons of water. Smaller amounts can be used in the same proportions. Slake the lime by pouring water over it. Mix the sulphur into a thin paste and, while the lime is slaking, pour it in, stir rapidly, add water and keep stirring. Have the caustic soda dissolved in water and stir it in with the lime and sulphur. This makes a reddish brown mixture, and when the proper amount of water is added it may be sprayed in the house or scrubbed on with a brush or broom. It is a biting wash, and will burn the skin where it touches, but it is sure death to lice, and will hold its killing power for weeks. It is far better than common whitewash, either lime alone or with carbolic acid. A few sprayings with this wash will kill out the mites and give the hens comfort.

BODY LICE.—These are larger insects that remain upon the hen, the eggs being laid on the feathers. They are not so dangerous as the mites, for a healthy hen provided with a good "dust bath" will get rid of most of them. When hens become feeble or unable to dust, the body lice do great damage. Some of the larger breeds do not use the dust bath regularly, and their feathers are thick and heavy. In Winter some poultrymen go so far as to warm the dusting box by using an iron bottom with a lamp under it. Lime mixed with the dust helps destroy the lice, but takes the gloss from the plumage. "Insect powder," tobacco dust or sulphur dusted through the feathers destroy the lice. There are several devices for dusting hens rapidly. One of them works like a barrel churn. The hen is put inside with a quantity of powder and turned over and over several times so that the powder works all through her feathers. Grease or fat will destroy the lice. A mixture of lard and sulphur, or equal parts of lard and kerosene smeared under the wings, around the vent and on the head and neck will protect the hen. The head lice which attack little chicks are overcome by smearing with lard and sulphur, butter or even cream, but as is stated elsewhere, the chick may be killed if too much grease is used. We give some space to the question of vermin, but it is an important one. Lice are probably responsible for more poultry failures than any other single trouble. With a fair use of insect powder and the lime and sulphur wash this fearful loss may be prevented.

TONICS FOR POULTRY.

When fowls are doing well it is not usually good policy to stimulate them with drugs of any kind. A legion of nostrums in the way of "egg foods" and "condition powders" has been offered poultry keepers from time to time. While there may be a small measure of merit in some of them all probably do more harm than good in the long run. Good general care, intelligent feeding and keen observation of the immediate needs of each fowl are the keynotes of success in poultry culture. There are times, however, when fowls, young and old, languish or lose the keen edge of their appetites and others when it seems advisable to force egg production to the utmost that simple remedies, between food and medicine, in their effects may be really useful. A few notes on the best of these tonics are appended.

RED PEPPER.—The red or cayenne pepper of commerce is made of the pungent fruit of Capsicum, or the common garden pepper ground to powder. It is an excellent appetizer, and probably the safest of all stimulants. It may be given in mashes or moist food at the rate of one teaspoonful to each two or more quarts. The fruits of any of the hot-flavored chilies or garden peppers answer equally well if broken up and added to the mash.

TINCTURE OF IRON.—In some forms of weakness associated with loss of appetite tincture of chloride of iron does good service. It should be given in the drinking water, 10 to 20 drops to the quart of water, given fresh for several successive days. It is rather caustic, but not poisonous in small quantities.

STRYCHNINE is a dangerous poison, but in minute doses has powerful tonic properties. It is especially useful in leg weakness and all forms of paralysis, and in the general depression following illness. It is best given fowls in the form of tincture of nux vomica, of which it is the active principle. Ten to 15 drops in a quart of drinking water may be safely given on alternate days. Nux vomica tincture is intensely bitter, and the water thus prepared is not relished.

ARSENIC is a powerful tonic and probably stimulates egg production. It may be given in the form of Fowler's solution, 10 to 12 drops in a quart of water once in three days. Nux vomica tincture and Fowler's solution are dangerous poisons and should be kept where children and animals cannot get at them.

GOLDEN SEAL.—An excellent appetizer very little used is golden seal or Hydrastis canadensis. It is harmless, and may be given at the rate of half an ounce of the powdered root to each quart of mash. Powdered ginger is also used in the same manner.

THE MOULTING HEN.—As all know poultry shed or cast off their feathers, after which a new growth appears. This moulting is an exhausting process, and the hen will not, under ordinary circumstances, lay during her moult or for some time after. Old hens drop their feathers during late Summer and Fall, and it is an advantage to force the moult early, so as to have them laying or at least in good condition before Winter sets in. Various plans have been tried for hurrying the moult. In some cases the feathers are plucked from the live hens so that a new growth will start early. Another plan often mentioned is described as follows by Mr. G. H. Belding:

"I took 10 White Wyandotte yearlings about the last of August and shut them up in a pen, and did not feed them for twelve days, with the exception of about a handful of grain every other day. I gave them all the water they wanted during these twelve days. At the expiration of 12 days I let them out, and commenced feeding a heavy ration, all they would eat, in fact giving them a variety, and once a day a mash and also beef scrap or animal meal. They had grass in the runs. Eight of them commenced to moult in a very short time. They laid on their new coat very fast, and were laying again in about six or seven weeks from the time I began. These hens were laying at the time the experiment began. They laid through the Winter and are still laying. One of the 10 it did not seem to affect; she moulted at the usual time, and did not begin laying until towards Spring. The other did not moult at all; she carried her old coat through the Winter and moulted this Spring. I did not give them any medicine or tonic."

Dark spots are often noticed in eggs. They are probably caused by the rupture of small blood vessels in the hen before the egg is shelled.

Bare backs on hens are caused by feather picking or by the male. When hens eat each other's feathers they usually pull out the soft down at the base of the tail. It is better to kill a confirmed feather puller. This bad habit is usually caused by idleness or lack of meat in the ration.

The egg shells may be crushed fine and fed to the hens. When crushed in this way they are not likely to cause egg eating.

The best cure for egg eating is to kill the hen that is guilty of it. We would do this except in the case of a valuable bird. By filing off the end of the beak we can prevent most of the trouble.

Leg weakness may be caused by rheumatism, a heavy male or roosts that are too high. Rheumatism is often caused by low damp quarters or by keeping the bird in a low coop on the ground.

A good hospital for a sick hen is at the bottom of a flour barrel in a nest of straw.

Soft-shelled eggs are mostly caused by a lack of lime. Crushed oyster shells or bone should be kept before the hens. Soft shells are also due to troubles in the reproductive organs, fright or shock or to the presence of too many males.

CHAPTER XVIII.

The Purebred Business Hen.

F. Q. White, who has met with much success as a breeder, gives the following good advice:

One of the questions continually asked by those thinking about trying to make poultry profitable is: "Would I not be just as successful with common fowls as with purebred or fancy stock? If not, why?" There are several reasons why it pays to keep purebred hens. First, your flock is uniform, and you can give the feed and care that your variety needs. With common mixed flocks you are feeding some hens fat, while others may not get what they need. Your chickens are much evener if all one kind, and if you are selling for broilers to a fancy trade, you would see a difference between a crate of nice purebred Wyandottes or Plymouth Rocks and a crate of red, white, blue and speckled scrubs. It might easily make a difference of two or three cents a pound. Now pick up the market quotations and note the prices on "fancy selected white" and the next grade, which means plain "fresh eggs." There you find a difference again of two or three cents a dozen. Does it cost any more to raise these fancy broilers or fancy eggs? Not a cent more after you get started. Of course it costs more to get a start in any purebred stock than in mongrels. Careful breeders have been at work for years developing these different breeds, each for a specific purpose, and it stands to reason that they will fulfill that purpose better than those with only hit or miss or no breeding.

We sometimes hear of some woman who is making money from common hens, but this only proves she understands her business and would make more if she had a good strain of purebred. It is a well-known fact that eggs of different breeds do not hatch alike, and some are much more difficult to hatch than others. One should take all these things into consideration and study the markets and their own likings, for anyone will make a much greater success with a breed he likes. After you have made your selection do not buy a male and try to grade up scrubs, and do not pay $25 for a show trio of fancy birds. First, get either a few settings or a hundred or more eggs of the breed you want from some breeder you can rely on to treat you fairly; then study your strain; find out its weak points, and buy males to correct those faults. This is when you want to buy a Standard and find what that breed should look like to win prizes. You will soon be proud of your flock and you will want to show all your friends your birds. If your hens are inclined to be too short-backed you should buy a male with the opposite tendency. If they are weak in any point get a male strong in that point to breed them to. But do not sacrifice vigor and health to fancy or fads; leave that to the showman. Don't try to keep more than one breed; you won't know all there is to know about that in 20 years. It is more profitable to be known as a good breeder of White Leghorns, Wyandottes or Plymouth Rocks than it is to be able to advertise one hundred different varieties of poultry for sale.

There is plenty of money in poultry if managed in a business-like manner. A dairyman would not keep Holstein cows for a fancy butter trade, nor would he expect to get rich from selling Jersey milk, although there are good butter cows and good milkers in both breeds. So a poultryman should keep the breed that is adapted to his business; the heavy breeds for market poultry and the lighter more active breeds for eggs. You will have hens in any breed that do not pay their board, and these must be weeded out and got rid of by the "ax process." It is a nice business to pick them out, and many a fine hen has been sacrificed because she was in such a ragged and generally dilapidated condition, due to her persistent laying. One trouble with scrubs is the lack of type and the extreme difficulty of culling out the unprofitable birds. We have all seen where good breeds that have been bred for years true to type were crossed. The result was a reversion and any old thing. Get purebred stock; keep it pure; strive to improve your strain constantly, and you will have a greater pride in your flock and give them better care, which after all is the secret of success in the poultry business. Who ever heard of a poultry man with some fine purebred hens allowing them to roost on the rail fence or over the pigpen? Take care of the hens and they will take care of you.

"PEDIGREE" HENS.—The "trap nests" mentioned on page 14 are not popular with most poultrymen, as they require much time and close attention. There is no doubt, however, that they can pick out the drones if they are operated carefully. At the Maine Experiment Station over 1,000 hens were tested. Out of this large number 35 hens were found that gave from 200 to 251 eggs in a year. There were several that laid only 36 to 60 eggs and three never laid at all. These hens were all selected because they looked like layers in shape and size, but the trap nests showed that the eye cannot be relied upon entirely. It has also been found that hens vary in their laying habits, some laying regularly month after month, while others lay well for a time and then take a vacation. These variations will be shown even when all are selected close to a "type."

CHAPTER XIX.

Who Should Keep Hens?

We have seen how the egg is formed, how it is hatched, how the little chick is cared for and how the hen is handled so as to make her a business proposition in feathers. Now, who should keep the Business Hen? Evidently a man should have "hen in the heart" if he expects Biddy to fill his pocket. From what we have studied we can readily see how much of the business side of the hen's work depends upon her partner man. Take a horse that will trot a mile in 2:10. Probably 30 seconds of that record is due to the man who trained and cared for the horse. Left to himself, with his natural gait, the horse could not trot under 2:40. The cow that produces an enormous weight of milk or butter is developed far beyond her natural flow by man's skill in handling and feeding. Just the same with the hen. There are records of flocks that average 160 eggs per year. Handled without skill or comfort such flocks would not average 60 eggs. That is why we said at the beginning that a man to succeed with the Business Hen must be "half hen' himself. While some will succeed better than others no one should think of investing money in the poultry business unless he is willing to put his heart into it and study the habits of the hens. There is money in the poultry business for those who do this.

HENS VS. COWS.—To show how the hen ranks as a financier, Geo. A. Cosgrove makes the following estimate. We do not disparage the value of good cows, but we cannot all be dairymen, and there is a larger surplus of milk than of fresh eggs:

"A neighbor (as we call them in the country, though he lives four miles away) keeps cows, I do not know how many, but he told me boastingly that his creamery check last month was $86 and his bill for grain $60. That leaves $26—a dollar a day—for profit, if he didn't have to feed any hay. Taking out the cost of hay for his 12 or 15 cows it would not leave a great deal for his month's work. Another farmer who keeps 30 cows, has a splendid farm, is a powerful man in the prime of life, and a worker, says that with the grain bill and hired help there is not a dollar in the cow business. He makes his own butter and sells it to private customers in a village six miles away. Hoard's Dairyman tells of two men who took a 'cow census.' In Pennsylvania 25 farmers who were patrons of a creamery averaged a net profit of $15.06 per year for each cow, while 25 more made a profit of 66 cents per cow. In Indiana the best *six* out of *fifty* averaged $21 per cow per year. It is fair to assume that these *best* cows were worth $45 to $60 each. Consequently it appears that it takes a good cow to pay an annual profit equal to one-third her market value.

"Now I rise to say that if there is anywhere in these United States any old dunghill, scaly-legged, blear-eyed, frosted-combed, roach-backed, crooked-breasted, twisted-toed apology for a hen, that with relative good care won't pay an annual profit on her market value of more than 33 per cent then she ought to be exhibited at the St. Louis Exhibition as the biggest curiosity in the show. I have kept fowls off and on for 40 years, in city and village back yards, and for the last 10 years on a farm, and I know there has never been a year when they did not pay me from 200 to 300 per cent on their market value."

PAID FOR A FARM.—Mr. Cosgrove knows what he is talking about, for the Wyandotte hen has paid for his home. He left the city at 57 years of age and invested all his savings in a run-down farm in a Connecticut hill town. There were 80 acres in the farm, with only 17 cleared, and barely two acres plowed. So poor was its reputation as a money earner that the farm sold for less than the cost of the buildings. It should be added that Mr. Cosgrove is in poor health, and has been unable to do a hard day's work in 10 years. He has been obliged to buy all his grain and figure close in every way. Yet, in spite of all these serious drawbacks the Wyandotte hens have paid for the farm twice over, and provided a good living. Mr. Cosgrove represents one class of men who should keep hens. No other stock could have come within the range of his powers and paid for his farm. He loved a hen, studied her needs and provided for them so well that his 400 hens give a gross income of over $3 each, besides giving meat and eggs for the family and fertilizer for the garden and fruit.

Mr. Cosgrove prefers Wyandottes for several good reasons. They are dignified without being dull. It takes a young and lively man to keep track of Leghorns. The Wyandottes will stay quietly inside a four-foot fence. They are thickly feathered, and do not require such warm housing as the more nervous breeds. Their combs are small—in fact head and comb can easily be put under the wing at night. Mr. Cosgrove says that if he were breeding Leghorns he would clip off their combs in the Fall about as Game cocks are trimmed. The wound would soon heal and the bird would suffer less from the cold. Mr. Cosgrove's experience shows what a man can do by selecting a breed or family with a definite performance in view. During the fearful Winter of 1904 his Wyandottes in their small and simple houses laid so well that they earned $20 a week clear of expenses. Of course, people heard of this and rightly thought that the character of the hens was largely responsible for it. As they could not hire Mr. Cosgrove to come and manage their poultry they were glad to pay a good price for part of his skill and care. Every hen on his farm and every egg that they lay will carry part of his skill in the shape of "pedigree," which we may call condensed performance. It always happens that when a careful man develops a flock of poultry so that they can earn more than the average, others are willing to pay extra for the stock. This reputation helps the sale of everything else that is grown on the farm.

BREEDING BUSINESS HENS.—The experience of C. H. Wyckoff, who became famous as a White Leghorn breeder, makes this point stronger. He started as a dairyman on a poor farm. There were 18 hens on the farm, which did little besides scratching up the garden. Mrs. Wyckoff had these hens put in a house with a yard and kept an account of eggs and food. They paid a profit of 75 cents a hen, and this gave Mr. Wyckoff an idea of what 500 good hens would do. He became satisfied that White Leghorns would pay him better, and so he got good specimens and began to study them and their needs. His case was quite different from that of Mr. Cosgrove. While the latter was an elderly man in poor health, Mr. Wyckoff was a young man, strong and vigorous, and with great capacity for work. While Mr. Cosgrove could raise no grain, Mr. Wyckoff could grow a large part of what was needed on his farm. I refer to this to show that the Business Hen suits all, the young, the old, the strong and the weak, provided they "love the hen." Six years after the 18 hens were put on record Mr. Wyckoff had 600 hens, which gave him a yearly income of $2,140, with a net profit of $1,070 after charging labor at $30 a month and interest on investment.

Mr. Wyckoff kept his hens in long yards or parks, growing plum or other fruit trees therein. This gave a double crop and left the farm free for a rotation of grain, hay and potatoes—the hens furnishing a good share of the manure required. Mr. Cosgrove also keeps his hens in yards, but makes no effort to cultivate the remainder of the farm. Mr. Wyckoff became a poultry expert. His careful study of the hen made him in time one of the most capable judges of Leghorns in the country. He never intended to go into the business of selling eggs for hatching; in fact he was quite annoyed when, after the story of his success was printed in THE R. N.-Y., people wanted to buy eggs and stock. The hens were paying well at providing eggs for eating purposes, but this very fact gave them an added value as breeders, and Mr. Wyckoff found that his hens had made him famous. Even the best of the young roosters, which were formerly sold as broilers, were easily sold at a dollar or more for breeders. This is always the experience of those who develop a good strain of poultry.

THE ENTIRE FARM.—Thus far we have discussed the plan thought best by many of yarding the hens on a small part of the farm and leaving the rest of the land idle or to be devoted to crop growing. The reverse of this plan is followed by O. W. Mapes, who tells us elsewhere about one day's work. Mr. Mapes has a pasture farm, rocky and in places quite thin.

His object is to save the expense of fencing and the "waiting on the hens" that is necessary when they are yarded. We get a good idea of his methods from his story. As between this plan and those followed by Mr. Cosgrove and Mr. Wyckoff there are arguments on both sides. Mapes saves the cost of fences, and in Summer the hens pick up nearly 40 per cent of their ration. One man, in Summer, can care for three times as many hens on this colony plan as he can when all are yarded. The great advantage of the yarding plan comes in Winter. It is a hard cold job to travel through deep snow to feed the hens in colony houses. The yard plan, with hens crowded together, is much better for the production of Winter eggs, which bring the highest price. It is not always true that the egg which brings the highest price per dozen is the most profitable egg, for it may cost too much to produce it. There is good profit in the Summer egg, even at a low price. The colony plan does not give as good a chance for selecting and breeding the best stock for breeders. In order to do that properly we must have some form of yard where the breeders can be kept by themselves. Mr. Mapes has been very succcessful with his hens, and his experience adds to the proof that a man who has "hen in his heart" can make poultry pay under any circumstances. For example, Mr. Hayward, of New Hampshire, makes his hens pay under conditions which most people would at first thought say are impossible. A brief outline of Mr. Hayward's plan is given on page 57 with a picture of one of his little houses. His 9,000 hens are kept in these little coops from the day they arrive as pullets till they are sold the next year as hens. The pullets are all bought from farmers, and are of no special breed. It is a hen-feeding farm, and the hens give an average profit of nearly one dollar each in spite of their close confinement. We cannot advise any such system for the average farmer, but it shows again how a careful man can take some breed of poultry and adapt it to any reasonable condition.

WITH A GARDEN.—Mr. Hartman tells us on page 73 how his hens provide Winter work on a truck farm. The experience of Alfred Johnson, of New Jersey, shows another side of poultry keeping. Mr. Johnson was a jeweler by trade. His eyes gave out, and instead of trying to find another job in town he bought 18 acres of land not far from Paterson, N. J., running in debt for the place. He studied his farm, and finally decided to make hens and strawberries his chief crops, with such other vegetables and fruits as would go with them. After 12 years work he sold in one year from his 18 acres $4,137.62 worth of produce. The 400 hens contributed nearly $800 worth of this in eggs, and also provided a good share of the fertilizer for the fruit. Of course, these hens were housed and fed with great care. They were kept clean and healthy. They are, of course, yarded since it would be impossible to give poultry a free run on a small fruit farm. After a time such yards become so foul that even plowing and growing pasture crops will not relieve them. The upper surface is scraped off and carried out to be used as manure, and fresh sand is brought back to take its place. Plum and pear trees are grown in the yards, giving considerable fruit. Mr. Johnson makes the most of the hen manure by mixing it with chemicals. It is kept hard and dry by dusting plaster under the perches. Twice a week the manure is removed and carried to a dry shed. In the Spring the hard chunks are spread out on a cement floor and pounded fine with a maul or heavy spade. It is then sifted, the coarse pieces being crushed again. Mr. Johnson mixes 400 pounds of sifted hen manure, 200 pounds dissolved bone black, 100 pounds muriate of potash and 150 pounds of plaster, and has a fertilizer which gives good results on his heavy and naturally rich soil. He uses large quantities of stable manure in addition, and this should be remembered by those who mix chemicals with hen manure. For most garden and fruit crops it would be necessary to use 200 pounds of nitrate of soda with the other chemicals. Mr. Johnson selected the Leghorn type of hen for his foundation stock because they are the best for laying large white eggs, which his market demands. He kept at first both Whites and Browns. The latter laid more eggs than the Whites, but the eggs were small. As an experiment Mr. Johnson began crossing the two breeds, and obtained chicks of all sorts of colors. Some of these cross-bred chicks were coal black, and as he liked their appearance Mr. Johnson saved the pullets and bred them to a pure Black Minorca rooster. As a result he has developed a strain of large black birds which are excellent layers. He has used a Black Minorca rooster most years and a Brown Leghorn twice without greatly changing the type of his hens. One flock of 270 hens averaged 160 eggs per year. Mr. Johnson had no desire to breed purebred poultry. He was simply after the hen that would lay the most eggs in Winter, for he has little time to give them in Summer. As is the case with all who develop a good flock, these black hens made such a reputation in the market that people wanted eggs for hatching. The pullets and even the young roosters are in demand for breeding stock. Strange to say, Mr. Johnson makes little use of incubators. These black hens will "sit," but they are poor nurses, and the little chicks are raised in brooders. The hens are marked with a toe punch which makes a hole on the web of the foot. One mark is made for each year of the hen's age. Two-year-old hens are used for breeders—about fifteen being put in a pen with a lively young cockerel. Mr. Johnson plans to use always purebred males. The three-year-old hens are fattened and sold, for Mr. Johnson thinks a hen yields like a strawberry plant. The best production is in the first year, but it is usually wise to fit up the hen and the berry field so as to run it another year.

I have known a number of people to start out with the idea of imitating Mr. Johnson's success. Most of them failed, and the reasons for their failure were quite evident to all but themselves. They underestimated their job, called it too easy and thought that success would follow without great exertion on their part. Some of them visited Mr. Johnson and saw how quietly and easily he went about his work. They copied his feeding methods and his plans for care, but they could not see that while their work was mechanical a thousand invisible forces were pulling with Mr. Johnson—things which he had gained in 20 hard years of experience. A man to succeed with poultry must have the patience of a sitting hen. In spite of all he can read or observe, or all the advice others can give him, the little chicks will die in the brooders. Many people grow discouraged at this loss, and quit the business. Then in the Fall, when the pullets are getting ready for laying, the expense for feeding is enormous and there is no income. It seems well-nigh impossible to fill up these greedy birds and the beginner who counts the cost without seeing the end is apt to grow frightened and slacken up on the feeding to save cost. He could not do a worse thing, for this will hold them back for weeks, and lose the value of Winter eggs. So the hen man needs a trunk full of patience and a bushel of faith, and we would not make the poultry business seem "too easy" to the beginner. Mr. Johnson has succeeded. The hens helped to pay for his home. They have given him a competence and now, since the death of his wife, carry him each year on a three-months' excursion to various parts of the world.

POULTRY FOR WOMEN.—I have heard a man tell how he ran away from a small New England farm when a boy because it seemed impossible to make it provide a simple living. He went back 20 years later expecting to find the place grown up to brush—abandoned. To his surprise he found the little farm prospering—neat and clean, with new buildings and conveniences in the house that he never heard of as a boy. As he expressed it, this had been brought about by "a hen and an old maid". A woman driven out of other employment had invested her savings in the farm. She had taken up poultry culture, and by good management and hard work had made the farm pay dividends which the former owners never thought possible. My friend's combination of "hen and old maid" has great possibilities, though married women and young girls are by no means barred. There are many cases where women have met with great success with poultry, though as a rule the business is harder for them than for men. They do such work as hatching, brooding and caring for the chicks better than men. We all know how as a last resort young stock that does not thrive with ordinary treatment is turned over to mother's care. The rougher work of cleaning houses, killing and dressing poultry, etc., is hard for a woman, and it is doubtful if she should attempt poultry keeping on a large scale without a stout boy or man to help her. On a farm where there are willing helpers, mother and the girls will often make a great success with the farm poultry. There are plenty of cases where such women have started with a poor flock of culls, and by wise selection and breeding developed a fine class of poultry that paid better than any other stock on the farm. Women can and will try many things for the comfort of stock which men would not think of. There has been considerable discussion as to whether it pays to provide artificial heat for hens. We may give here the experience of Zimmer Bros. who live in Cayuga Co., New York, a cold section.

"We have one poultry house, 30x60, which is divided into 12 pens and has an alley through the center of the house. We use a hot water heater and pipe system for heating it at a cost of $100 for the heating system. Last Winter we used one ton of coal to keep this building at a temperature of 35 to 40. We let the fire out when a thaw was on, and only ran it when the thermometer came to the freezing point inside the building, which was about half the time. This building is used for a brooder house during the Spring months, and this is when we get full value from our heating system by using the hot water pipes for brooders. We have another house, 20x50, divided into six pens with a stove in one end, and the smoke pipe running the whole length of house. One ton of coal has run this stove during the past cold Winter, keeping the inside temperature above freezing. Both these houses are lined, which makes the coal bill small, but when we build again we shall not line the house, because the lining is of no use except during two or three cold months, and the interest on the cost of lining will buy enough coal to keep the house from freezing, and we have severe Winters in this section."

The farm women can often do much to interest the boys in good poultry. Really a good flock of hens is better for a farmer's boy than a colt or calf. The hens will keep him busy, give money returns quicker and furnish more novelty. Where a woman can interest the boys and get them to help her care for the hens we have one of the best combinations that can be made on a farm.

CHAPTER XX.

Odds and Ends.

How much cut bone should be fed?

It depends upon what you feed with it. With corn alone or for most of the ration one ounce per hen each day will be safe. Less if meat or linseed is used in the mash.

How long should hens be kept for layers?

Depends upon the hen. Some hens will lay profitably at four years old, others are of little use after the second season. The majority of poultrymen sell ordinary hens when 2½ years old.

Will hens continue to lay when no male bird is kept with them?

Yes; better than when a crowd of surplus roosters are kept. We would keep no rooster except with the breeding hens.

Will infertile eggs keep longer than fertile ones?

Yes, in warm weather or in places where the eggs are heated. In cool weather there is little difference.

How long after the male is placed with the hens will the eggs become fertile?

Cases are on record where eggs laid 40 hours after the male was introduced hatched healthy chicks. The surest results are obtained after six or seven days.

How long after the male is taken away will the eggs remain fertile?

In some cases eggs laid two weeks after the male was removed have hatched. We must remember that hens vary greatly in this respect. Some rarely, if ever, lay eggs that will hatch, while others lay a large proportion of hatchable eggs. After a hen has been laying for a long time the eggs are less likely to be fertile than earlier in the season. The male pays greater attention to some hens than to others. This is one reason why the system of double males (page 27) pays.

How can we prevent fertile eggs from hatching and not injure them for sale?

Shake or jar the egg. Hold it in the right hand and strike at the other hand so as to shock the egg without breaking the shell. This breaks up the delicate membranes inside the egg and destroys its life.

Does a Leghorn hen ever become broody?

Yes, but few will sit through the period of incubation. They are so nervous that a little handling will break them of the desire. Few pure Leghorns are safe mothers.

HEN PASTURE.—Where there is land enough it pays to have partitions in the chicken yard so as to give pasture for the hens. A crop of Crimson clover in the Spring will provide 60 per cent of the hen's food while it lasts. Rape is excellent for hen feed, and a patch of it may be ready when the clover is done. Another small patch of oats may follow this, and the place where the Crimson clover grew may be sown to cow peas. After the oats are done this patch may be seeded to Crimson clover and turnips, thus keeping up a succession of green food.

DOUBLE CHICKEN YARDS.—Our henhouses are built so that they open into two large yards. The family garden is alternated back and forth between them. This year the hens run in what was last year's garden; next year they will be put where the garden is now. This plan is a good one where there is space enough for a large yard. The droppings of the hens are utilized and the soil is cleaned up and purified by cropping. On most of the garden soil it is possible to follow the last crop with Crimson clover or rye, which make good Spring pasture for the hens. These chicken yards are long and narrow. We find that it pays to go in with a horse and small plow frequently and turn the soil over. This gives the hens an abundance of worms and helps fit the ground for next year's garden.

CATCHING HENS.—The two devices shown herewith are useful to save chasing a hen and running her down. The upper one is like a small-sized shepherd's crook—a wooden handle with a bent wire attached. This wire can be reached out to catch the hen by the leg and hold her. The other is a good-sized fisherman's hand net with a long handle. With a little practice it becomes easy to catch the hen in this net.

POULTRY AS INSECTICIDES.—Poultry eat large quantities of insects when permitted free range. They are particularly fond of earthworms, grasshoppers and the like. We have never known hens to eat Squash bugs, or Potato beetles, though there are reports from good authorities that they have done so. We once kept a large flock of hens and chicks in a potato field, after the plants were about six inches high. They certainly ate many of the egg clusters of the Potato beetle, but, so far as we could see, none of the hatched insects. We have kept chickens in a cornfield with very good results. A well-known method of fighting the Asparagus beetle and the Onion maggot is to scatter coops with hens and young chickens over the field. In an orchard poultry consume many injurious insects, and greatly help the trees. Ducks are perhaps the best insect-killers of all domestic poultry. It is reported on good authority that they will eat Potato beetles, Army worms and even chinch bugs. In tobacco and cotton fields overrun with grass geese have been used to help weed the crop. They will eat a fair share of the grass and leave the cotton and tobacco.

TRAINING AN EGG EATER.—A man sees an empty orange crate in the village store, and says to the grocer: "Give me that, will you? It's just what I want for a couple of hen's nests." He takes it home and nails it up in the henhouse, putting two inches or so of straw in the bottom. The hens like that nest and lay six or eight eggs in it; the next hen that jumps down into the nest is a heavy one, and her toe smashes an egg. As she turns to cuddle the eggs under her she sees the most delicious morsel that a hen has ever tasted, plunges her beak into it, and greedily sucks it up; then eats the shell and begins to scratch to get the last particle of it, throwing the eggs against the side of the box and perhaps breaking another, which is also eaten. Next day she goes to scratching again in the nest, remembering what a treat she found there, and breaks another egg, and now your confirmed egg eater is formed. The remedy, in the case of that hen, is to cut off her head. But prevention is much better; have no nest that a hen has to *jump down* into. Fill all nests to within four inches of top, so the hens can step from the edge into the nest, and the liability of having egg eaters in the flock will be very much lessened.

POULTRY PESTS.—Hawks capture many chicks. A good marksman can kill a few and hang them on poles about the yards. A southern remedy is to mix strychnine in molasses and rub a little on the top of each small chicken. The hawk is supposed to poison himself while eating the chick! Guinea hens alarm the neighborhood when hawks are near. The best remedy is to keep the little chicks in covered runs until they are large enough to run for shelter. It is well to have low-growing shrubs about where the chicks can hide. Cats have caused us great damage, which we have mostly avoided by keeping the little birds in covered yards. If pigs run in the field with the chicks they must be carefully watched. If a pig once gets a taste of chicken he will chase the birds constantly. Rats and larger wild animals, like minks, are sworn enemies of little chicks. They can only be kept out of the brooders by making them rat-proof, lifted above the ground with no chance for the rat to climb. Cement floors and stone foundations are particularly useful in poultry houses, because the rats cannot work into them. In some cases rats congregate in the barn in great numbers, and cats and traps are powerless to keep them down. In such cases poisons are used. A cake made of cornmeal and bran, with a quantity of white arsenic mixed in, is baked much the same as a biscuit, and crumbs of it are scattered about the building. It usually does the business, but the hens must be shut up and the cats and other domestic animals kept away from the barn while this poison is about.

POULTRY MANURE.—Some people have extravagant ideas about the value of hen manure, calling it worth as much as Peruvian guano. It has no such value, as a little thought will show. The manure which forms the guano comes from birds that live mostly on fish and meat. The bodies of dead birds are also mixed with it. The hen lives mostly on grain or food that other farm stock eat, and we can easily see there can be no fertilizing value to the manure except what comes from the food. An average sample of hen manure without too much litter or sand in it is worth about four times as much as an equal weight of cow manure. This is because the excrement from the kidneys is passed with the solids, while with other farm animals it is separated and largely lost. Hen manure contains a large proportion of nitrogen, and, if used alone, gives best satisfaction on crops that make most of their growth above ground, like corn, cabbage or vegetables. Where there is but a small quantity it can be kept in barrels, spread in the Spring and worked into the garden soil. On large poultry farms it is often successfully used for mixing with chemicals to make a fertilizer. Plaster or acid phosphate alone or mixed with sawdust is sprinkled under the perches so as to keep the manure dry and free from fermentation. As often as need be it is raked off the platform and stored in a dry shed. In the Spring it will be found in dry hard lumps, which are crushed as fine as possible, usually by beating them on a hard floor with heavy shovels. The following mixture gives good results for many crops: 1,000 pounds sifted hen manure, 500 pounds acid phosphate, 200 pounds muriate of potash and 300 pounds of fine ground bone. Do not use lime under the roosts nor mix it with the manure long before it is put into the soil, for the lime starts a chemical action which sets free the ammonia. The plaster or the acid phosphate may be used under the roosts, because they stop this escape of ammonia. Hen manure and wood ashes may be put together in the soil, but should not be mixed and left above ground. The custom followed by many farmers of putting a handful of pure hen manure in and around each hill of corn is a good one, for such manure is especially useful for corn.

PRESERVING EGGS.—It is often desirable to carry eggs through several months or a year. Most hens persist in laying most of their eggs through Spring and early Summer. In late Summer and Winter eggs are scarce and high in price. If one can take eggs worth 15 cents a dozen and hold them so that they will be fresh and good when the price is 40 cents he has a good business proposition. In the large cities this is done by putting the eggs in cold storage, but this is impossible on the farm. Formerly such eggs were kept fairly well in lime water, but this gave a brittle shell and many of the eggs were "musty." The most practical way of preserving eggs is to keep them dipped in a solution of water glass or silicate of soda. This water glass can be bought at most drug stores or from large manufacturers. To use it the solution is placed in a wooden or stoneware vessel, and nine times the quantity of fresh pure water poured in. The eggs are placed in the liquid when gathered, as fresh as possible, only allowing them to cool off. Put in as many eggs as the solution will cover. Cover with a lid to retard evaporation and keep out dust. Store in a cool cellar until wanted for use. The eggs should keep perfectly at least one year. The eggs *must* be sound and fresh when placed in the solution—it will not restore stale or spoiled specimens. One pound of water glass properly diluted will cover about 14 dozens of eggs. We have used the same solution two years in succession with good results, but it is probably best to start each season with a fresh supply. The only change to be noted in eggs preserved one year in a 10-per-cent solution is that the white or albumen is rather more watery than in perfectly fresh eggs. They closely resemble new-laid eggs in appearance and quality after being rinsed and dried off. They are useful for all culinary purposes except boiling in the shell, as they are likely to crack if heated too suddenly and the interior does not look quite as inviting when opened. Repeated trials have since convinced us that these eggs keep well for two weeks after coming out of the solution if stored in a cool place, and are even better for some purposes, as the white becomes less watery. This does not warrant offering water-glassed eggs as fresh, however. They are preserved eggs, and should be so called if offered for sale. As a household economy for the storage of eggs when cheap and plentiful the water-glass process is to be heartily commended. With a stock of well-preserved eggs packed in April and May available for family use during the succeeding cold months the farmer or poultry keeper is at liberty to sell his Winter product as laid. This method is for home consumption and not for eggs to be sold as "fresh."

A FAMILY FLOCK.—H. H. Boardman, of Connecticut, says: "For about 30 years I have kept small flocks of Black Spanish, Brahmas, White and Brown Leghorns, Plymouth Rocks, and White Wyandottes. For value I would reverse the order of above list. The Plymouth Rocks are fine fowls. As Winter layers they are only excelled by White Wyandottes, and that but slightly. But they have some defects. They are too large. I had a yearling cockerel weighing 11¾ pounds; a couple of two-year-old hens 10 pounds each. My friend the butcher prefers those of six to eight pounds. They sell better, he says. Their single combs in extremely cold weather often becomes frostbitten, which stops their laying. Finally, they are the only breed with me that have been troubled with rheumatism, where the others under like conditions have not been at all affected. The White Wyandottes, while not perfect, seem to combine more good qualities than any breed I have tried. Averaging five to eight pounds, they seem to be about the right weight for the table. For laying, however, best results come from pullets—65 to 70 per cent for December, January and February. Two-year-old hens, on account of late moulting and early cold weather, dropped this past Winter to 10 or 15 per cent, which is much smaller than previous years, so it would seem to be more profitable to keep more pullets and fewer old hens. Another difficulty I find in propagating; chickens that get out of the shell are hardy and healthy, but percentage is small, 25 to 50 per cent. Eggs from pullets seem to hatch much better than from two-year-old hens. Perhaps the redundancy of eggs during the Winter months causes weakness and thus impairs reproductive qualities of the eggs. This year breeding from pullets gave 65 chicks from 12 sittings; last year breeding from two-year-old hens, 25 chicks from nine sittings. There has been much complaint about poor hatching of Wyandotte eggs.

"In feeding chicks after first few days, I give cracked corn and wheat early in the morning, mash of middlings and cracked corn about nine o'clock, wetted with skim-milk; corn and wheat again at noon; more mash about three; more corn and wheat just before sundown. Fresh water, a little fresh meat, grass or green food go without saying. Others may have a better system, but I find chicks thrive on this, and seldom lose one unless by accident.

"I have two houses for hens with about one-eighth acre yard to each. No. 1 house, 7 x 12, walls of matched boards, ceiling and walls lathed and plastered, one window facing south and one west. No. 2 house, 9 x 16, walls of matched boards, unlined, four windows facing south, that side being practically all glass; cost to build about two-thirds that of No. 1. Both houses are without floors, the earth bottom being covered with litter and location dry. Winter of 1902-3 10 two-year-old hens in No. 1 house laid in December, January and February 441 eggs, 44.01 per hen. Same months of 1903-4 18 two-year-old hens in No. 1 house laid 160 eggs, 8.99 per hen. This great disparity may be attributed to late moulting, early cold weather, and too many hens in narrow quarters. Other conditions were substantially the same. In house No. 2, in December, January and February, 1902-3, 19 May pullets laid 1,030 eggs, 54.2 per hen. Same months of 1903-4 13 May pullets laid 651 eggs, 50.1 per pullet. Two of the coldest days of Winter, January 4 and 5, when the temperature dropped to 33 degrees below zero here, the 13 pullets laid 19 eggs. When the temperature was 20 degrees or above the doors of both houses remained open during the day, and hens came outside most of the day when the ground was bare. Warm mash was composed of wheat middlings, cracked corn, ground beef scraps, ground oyster shells, moistened with skim-milk and hot water in the morning. Add once or twice a week a little powdered charcoal and cut bone. At noon give a little of the mash with remnants from the table; at night whole corn, wheat and oats; cabbage and cut clover occasionally."

INDEX

	PAGE.
Bantam Breeding	96
Barns for Hens	56
Breeds, American	6
Asiatics	8
Business	5
Crossing	16
Mediterranean	5
Breeders, Care of	15
Breeding to Type	81, 82
Broilers, Coop of	85
"Squab"	47
Brooder, Homemade	36
Houses	38
Brooders, Clean	39
Chicken Bread	43
Coops	41
Yards, Double	121
Chick, Baby, Care of	40
Chicks, Helping Out of Shell	34
How Mapes Feeds	44
Cholera	103
Cockerels, Keep Separate	46
Cold Storage	87
Colony Plan	68, 69, 70, 71, 72
Crate for Live Poultry	83
Disease Prevention	98
Diseases, Hereditary	98
Drinking Fountain	66
Ducks	96, 97
Egg Eater, Training	122
How Made	18
Packages	90
Parts of	19
Parents of	13
Sex of	28
Shipment, Regular	91
Time Required to Produce	26
What is?	18
Eggs, Fancy Market for	88
Forms of	23, 24, 25
From Table Scraps	77
Incubator Testing	30
Preserving	123
Uniform for Hatching	28
Feeding, Correct	98
Devices	67
Various Methods of	60, 61, 62, 63
Fence, Wire	100
Flock, Family	124
Scrub, Improving	11
Floor Materials	55
Food Stuffs, Analysis of	59
Foods, Muscle-making Needed	65
Gapes	104
Guinea Fowl	93
Hen, Broody	29
Broody, Breaking Up	32
Catching	121
Cosgrove's	114
Dust Box	55

	PAGE.
Hen House, Warming	53
For Hatching	30
House Interiors	51, 52
House, Old, Repairing	12
House, Sanitary	99
House, Essentials For	49
Johnson's	117
Non-Sitters	5
On Truck Farm	116
Pasture	121
Pedigree	112
Scrub	10
Should Lay Young	45
Sitting, How Cosgrove Handles	30
Vs. Cows	113
Wyckoff's	115
Young, Care of	45
Incubation, What Is	29
Incubators, Handling	32
Influenza	99
Kerosene Emulsion	107
Layer, Selecting	13
Leghorns, Brown	6
White	6
Lice	105
Lime and Sulphur Wash	108
Mangels as Feed	43
Market Gardener's Hens	73, 74, 75
Marketing Poultry Products	83
Meat Shop, Jewish	84
Minorcas, Black	6
Moulting, Hastening	109
Nests, Trap	14
Pedigree	13
Pigeons and Squabs	94
Plymouth Rock, Origin of	6
Special Features of	7
Poultry as Insect Killers	121
For Women	118
Killing	86
Manure	123
Pests	122
Purebred, Advantage of	111
Ration, Balanced	58
Maintenance	66
Rhode Island Red	6
Roost, Swinging	56
Roosts, Best Form of	56
Roosters, How Many for Flock	27
Roup	101
Scaly Leg	104
Scratching Shed Arrangement	53
Selection, C. H. Wyckoff on	13
Shell and Grit Box	50
Surgical Treatment	105
Tonics	108
Turkeys, Care of	95
Wyandotte, White, Value of	8
Yards, Treatment of	101

Printed in Great Britain
by Amazon